MEDGAR EVERS

Jennie Brown

MELROSE SQUARE PUBLISHING COMPANY
LOS ANGELES, CALIFORNIA

Consulting Editors for Melrose Square
Raymond Friday Locke
James Neyland

Cover Painting: Jesse Santos
Cover Design: Bill Skurski

MEDGAR EVERS

MELROSE SQUARE
BLACK AMERICAN SERIES

ELLA FITZGERALD
singer
NAT TURNER
slave revolt leader
PAUL ROBESON
singer and actor
JACKIE ROBINSON
baseball great
LOUIS ARMSTRONG
musician
SCOTT JOPLIN
composer
MATTHEW HENSON
explorer
MALCOLM X
militant black leader
CHESTER HIMES
author
SOJOURNER TRUTH
antislavery activist
BILLIE HOLIDAY
singer
RICHARD WRIGHT
writer
ALTHEA GIBSON
tennis champion
JAMES BALDWIN
author
JESSE OWENS
olympics star
MARCUS GARVEY
black nationalist leader
SIDNEY POITIER
actor
WILMA RUDOLPH
track star
MUHAMMAD ALI
boxing champion
FREDERICK DOUGLASS
patriot & activist
MARTIN LUTHER KING, JR.
civil rights leader
ZORA NEALE HURSTON
author
SARAH VAUGHAN
singer

HARRY BELAFONTE
singer & actor
JOE LOUIS
boxing champion
MAHALIA JACKSON
gospel singer
BOOKER T. WASHINGTON
educator
NAT KING COLE
singer & pianist
GEORGE W. CARVER
scientist & educator
WILLIE MAYS
baseball player
LENA HORNE
singer & actress
DUKE ELLINGTON
jazz musician
BARBARA JORDAN
congresswoman
GORDON PARKS
photographer & director
MADAME C.J. WALKER
entrepreneur
MARY MCLEOD BETHUNE
educator
THURGOOD MARSHALL
supreme court justice
KATHERINE DUNHAM
dancer & choreographer
ELIJAH MUHAMMAD
religious leader
ARTHUR ASHE
tennis champion
A. PHILIP RANDOLPH
union leader
W.E.B. DU BOIS
scholar & activist
DIZZY GILLESPIE
musician & bandleader
COUNT BASIE
musician & bandleader
HENRY AARON
baseball player
MEDGAR EVERS
social activist

CONTENTS

Chapter One

June 12, 1963

MIDNIGHT. QUIET REIGNS in a middle-class, mostly black neighborhood in Jackson, Mississippi. Small, ranch-style brick houses are lined up in neat rows on both sides of the street. Late-model cars are parked in the driveways. The neighborhood exudes peace and contentment, like most suburbs. This is a place where nothing could go wrong. Or so it seems.

A person walking down this street would see no sign that Jackson, Mississippi, was far from the most peaceful place on earth at this time. It was shaping up to be another long, hot summer in the ongoing war for civil rights for black

Medgar Evers, the Mississippi NAACP field secretary, was gunned down as he arrived home from a meeting on the night of June 12, 1963, an act that shocked both blacks and whites.

southerners. The previous month, hundreds of young blacks—many of them high school students—had been arrested and jailed for protesting racial segregation in the schools. Allen Thompson, the mayor of Jackson, refused to hear complaints of the Mississippi branch of the National Association for the Advancement of Colored People (NAACP) about the lack of black workers in city jobs. White racists lurked in the background, eager to slay any "crazy nigger" who threatened their way of life. Racial tension was at a dangerously high level.

But here on Guynes Street, no one was fighting tonight.

A few minutes later came the gunshot—the shot that rocked not only Jackson but the entire nation.

Medgar Evers, age thirty-seven, the field secretary for the NAACP's Mississippi branch, stepped out of his 1962 Oldsmobile after returning from a meeting at New Jerusalem Baptist Church. Before he could reach his front door, Evers was shot in the back with a high-powered rifle blast. The bullet came out with such velocity that it pierced a window and an interior wall before ending up in the kitchen of the Evers house. The gunman, hiding in a honeysuckle thicket, abandoned his weapon and fled immediately.

Myrlie Evers, Medgar's wife, and their three

Jackson, Mississippi. In Medgar Evers' time the city was a hotbed of racism, but the years have brought a welcome change. "Jackson has problems with crime and gangs, like any city, but it's a good place to live," said a Jackson State professor.

young children were awakened by the shot. Myrlie opened the front door to find her husband lying face-down in a growing puddle of blood, still holding his keys. She screamed and knelt down to lift his head. The three children cried, "Please, Daddy, please get up!" He didn't. He was still breathing, but his open eyes were unmoving and glazed. He opened his mouth in an attempt to speak, but no sound came out. This was a man who needed help fast.

Regaining her senses, Myrlie went back into the house and called the police. The neighbors were already slowly swarming toward the Evers house. Myrlie saw white faces among them, and never before had white faces seemed so dangerous to her. "I don't think I have ever hated as much in my life as I did at that moment anyone who had white skin," she wrote later. "I can recall wanting...to have a machine gun or something in my hands, and to stand there and mow them all down."

Evers was placed upon his daughter Rena's mattress and rushed to the University of Mississippi Hospital in neighbor Houston Wells' station wagon. There was no time to call an ambulance. On the way to the hospital, Evers reportedly said, "Sit me up..., turn me loose." A bullet in the back could not stop this man's fighting spirit.

At home, Myrlie Evers got down on her knees

Byron de la Beckwith was arrested and charged with the murder of Medgar Evers. At the time he was tried twice, but both resulted in hung juries. In 1994, he was tried again and convicted.

in the living room and prayed, not that her husband's life would be saved, but that she would have the strength to endure whatever the Lord brought. An encouraging report came over the phone that Medgar had regained consciousness. But that condition was not to last.

Hattie Tate, another neighbor, came into the Evers house and told Myrlie all that she needed to know without words. Medgar Evers was dead, the latest in a long line of blacks who had been killed because they knew that the "way things were" in the South were not the way things ought to be—and tried to do something about it.

After informing her aunt and Medgar's brother Charles, Myrlie went across the street to Jean Young's house, where the children were temporarily sheltered. When she came back to the Evers house, the yard was filled with neighbors—and the police, who had finally arrived.

Myrlie was furious. The all-white Jackson police force was the only law enforcement in town, and it was a well-known fact that it was no friend of the black community. Some of these same policemen had stalked her husband, tried to run him over in their squad car, and looked upon the Everses' complaints with skepticism. As they poked around the crime scene, Myrlie screamed, "Get off my property!" At this moment, she blamed all whites for Medgar's

Mayor Allen Thompson of Jackson. The morning following the assassination of Medgar Evers, he offered a five-thousand-dollar reward on behalf of the city and the city commissioners.

murder. "Is a Negro's blood any different? Do you think that by killing him you can put an end to what he's been doing? You'll have to kill me and a lot of other Negroes first."

Dr. A.B. Britton, the Evers family physician, had been at the hospital where Medgar died. He returned to comfort Myrlie.

"I couldn't treat him, you know," he said, referring to yet another ridiculous example of race segregation, "because it was a white hospital, but I saw that they did everything they could." When he thought the white doctors were moving too slowly, Dr. Britton was compelled to inform them, "This man is Medgar Evers, field secretary of the NAACP."

"Oh, my God," said one of them.

News of the assassination swiftly reached the people of Mississippi, both black and white. It ignited a new round of protest. "Every one of us [blacks] is mad," said a Jackson resident, "and that's an understatement."

By the next morning, grieving blacks from all walks of life peacefully marched in the streets of Jackson and were met with the usual arrests and police brutality. The marches and arrests lasted for more than a week.

Mississippi Governor Ross Barnett said, "Apparently, it was a dastardly act, and as governor...I shall cooperate in every way to apprehend the guilty party. Too many incidents are

World War II African-American soldiers. A combat veteran of that war, Evers said, "If I die, it will be in a good cause," in comparing his civil rights activities to those of wartime combat.

happening throughout the country...."

Mayor Thompson offered a five-thousand-dollar reward for the assassin and added, "The commissioners [of Jackson] and I are dreadfully shocked, humiliated, and sick at heart that such a terrible tragedy should happen in our city." Thompson conveniently ignored his own stubbornness regarding segregation and the criminal behavior of his own police department.

As the politicians expressed the proper outrage, others were frankly pleased. A white man, drinking at a local bar, was quoted as saying, "Maybe this will slow the niggers down."

Not by a long shot.

Medgar Evers knew full well that wherever a civil rights activist walked—especially in Mississippi—death was never far behind. Ever since 1955, a year after he became the NAACP's first field secretary in Mississippi, Evers' name was on a "death list" that circulated among white racists. Death threats constantly made their way to the Evers house, and there had been an attempt to firebomb the house shortly before the assassination.

But through all of this, Evers refused to turn his back on the effort to free southern blacks from decades of repression, knowing that what he was fighting for was more important than even his own life. "If I die, it will be in a good cause," said this World War II combat veteran.

"I've been fighting for America just as much as soldiers in Vietnam."

The civil rights struggle of the fifties and sixties was indeed every bit as much a war as anything that happened in Vietnam. There was danger, blood, pain, terror—and casualties like Medgar Evers.

What made Evers and his compatriots wage war with a well-entrenched tradition of southern racism, despite impossible odds? Perhaps it was because they knew that they were not only fighting for the basic dignity that white citizens enjoyed, but for survival for themselves and their descendants.

Today, blacks in all fifty U.S. states enjoy freedoms that their ancestors could only dream of. The degradations of the past read like horror fiction today. Unfortunately, those who lived through it could never close the book and go to sleep. It was truly a waking nightmare.

Imagine having to use a separate restroom from the rest of the general population. Imagine losing your job or your mortgage simply because you registered to vote. Imagine hearing your grandfather being called "boy." Imagine walking miles to your school, in good weather and bad, while others rode a bus—only to receive a substandard education, thus limiting your opportunities for employment. Imagine stepping onto a bus and having the driver tell you to go to the

Mississippi Governor Ross Barnett leads the cheers as the Ole Miss Rebels win their 1962 homecoming game over the University of Houston by a score of 40-7. The game was moved to Jackson from Oxford by order of the Defense Department

following the riots of the prieviousweekend over the registration of James Meredith from traditional black Jackson State College. Ross and Alabama's George Wallace and Arkansas' Orval Faubus were fervent in their opposition to integration.

back—even though the back is standing-room-only and there are plenty of empty seats up front. Imagine having to be extremely careful about how you behave among the same people who oppress you—one "uppity" word, one sign of protest during the day could get you lynched that night. Imagine being beaten or raped, or having a relative or friend murdered, and knowing that the perpetrator will never be arrested, let alone convicted and jailed. Imagine a world where your self-esteem and your pride are destroyed every day—simply because of the color of your skin.

That was Mississippi when Medgar Evers became NAACP field secretary in 1954. With superhuman drive and patience, he recruited thousands of new NAACP members, encouraged blacks to take advantage of the ballot box despite white opposition, and gave a people a voice to express itself. "If we can get rid of our sense of inferiority," he said, "we can begin to win our equality peacefully."

Evers may have lost his life before his work was finished, but no one could assassinate his influence. By 1965, desegregation was complete in Mississippi and blacks could vote without fear.

The right to vote, the right to a decent education, the right to be treated as a citizen and a human being—those basic rights are what

Medgar Evers wanted to win for his people. Before "Black Power" and Afrocentrism must come knowledge, economic power, and the means and courage to improve one's world. Although Evers is less-known than other civil rights heroes such as Martin Luther King, his impact was no less important or lasting.

Says Benjamin Hooks, the current Executive Director of the NAACP: "Medgar Evers' place in history rests not on service on foreign fields against a foreign foe, but in service and leadership in the war at home for the soul of America. His is a story that must be told and retold. Too few young people know his story, and that is a tragedy greater than his untimely death."

Chapter Two

Beginnings

Decatur, MISSISSIPPI, where Medgar
Wiley Evers was born on July 2, 1925, was a
typical southern farming community. It was
broiling in summer yet rainy in winter, provid-
ing a fertile deep brown soil that gave rewards
to those who worked it. Because this was
Mississippi, however, the town had two separate
lives—white and black. The races intersected for
business and, occasionally, in regard to community matters.

Medgar—named after a great-grandfather
who had been a slave—was the second child of
James and Jessie Evers. The Everses lived in a

---

*While schools and churches were segregated, the whites and
blacks of the South in Medgar Evers' time intersected for business and, occasionally, in regard to community matters.*

frame house on the edge of town, and they possessed a patch of farmland and some farm animals such as cows, pigs, and chickens. Yet the family could not live on farming alone. So James took intermittent jobs at the railroad and sawmill, and Jessie, like many of her peers, worked as a domestic for a white family and took in ironing (for fifty cents per twenty shirts).

When the children—Charles, Elizabeth, Medgar, and Ruth, plus three older children from Jessie's previous marriage—were old enough, they, too, were expected to work. Charles and Medgar had many imaginative ways to earn extra cash, such as picking up scrap metal and empty soda bottles. The family was never so poor as to starve, but they always had to scramble and economize to make ends meet. The Everses were justifiably proud of their self-sufficiency and were respected in both the black and white communities.

James Evers was a tall, tough man who didn't take guff from anyone—at home or outside. He was the only black man in Decatur who refused to step down from the sidewalk when white people approached. Other blacks would have at least received a severe reprimand, but not James Evers. Just one look proved to all that this was not a man to trifle with. Sometimes, however, appearance was not enough.

Once, Mr. Evers took Charles and Medgar to

Virtually every county courthouse in the South has a statue of a Confederate soldier in front of it, a focus of malcontent for many modern blacks. However, it is difficult to rewrite history.

the sawmill commissary, or general store. Despite not being able to read or write, Mr. Evers was excellent at figures and immediately noticed that he was overcharged on the bill. The white store owner refused to believe it.

"You calling' me a liar, nigger?" he demanded.

When Mr. Evers insisted that the bill was wrong, the white man, feared for his brutality towards blacks, stepped behind the counter for his gun.

Mr. Evers grabbed a soda bottle, smashed it, and pointed the jagged edge at the white man. "If you move another step, I'll bust your brains out," he warned.

A crowd of whites had gathered around the scene, but none of them intervened. The store owner, now frightened, did not move.

The three Everses retreated from the store. Miraculously, none of the whites retaliated. Blacks had been murdered in Mississippi for far less provocation.

"Don't never let any white folks beat you," Mr. Evers told his sons afterward. "If anyone ever kicks you, beat the hell out of him."

This confrontation taught Medgar that racists, at heart, were cowards because they were afraid of the unknown. It also showed that passivity was not the only possible response to injustice. For that alone, Mr. Evers earned his place as one of his son's heroes.

Medgar Evers was born in the small east central Mississippi
town of Newton on July 2, 1925. He attended the nearby one-
room county school, finishing Newton High after military service.

Jessie Evers, too, was strong. She not only had to run her own household but those of several white families as well. Sometimes, she got only a few hours of sleep per night. It was hardly an enviable life, but it was not as degrading as it could have been. White employers depended upon their black domestics and gave them some respect and wages. Charles later said in his autobiography that "the only people in Mississippi who have freedom are the white man and the black woman."

Mrs. Evers' patient attitude came from her religion. She was a member of the Church of God in Christ, a Baptist sect that required unusual devotion from its members. The Evers family attended church three days a week in addition to Sunday services—which lasted all day long. Medgar was exposed to hours of hymns, testimonials, and preaching.

A casual observer might find this attention to religion obsessive. But that was not the case here. The church was one of the few solaces for southern blacks in a hostile world. Church was the one place where blacks could gather without arousing white suspicion. The whites did not interfere in black religion, believing that it kept blacks humble and subservient. They did not know that the black church would someday become one of the roots of the civil rights movement, as the disparity between Christian values of peace and brotherhood and institutionalized racism became clear.

Charles noticed that "a lot of young people resent the church because it's always promising heaven in the sweet bye and bye and lulling black people into accepting a subhuman way of life here on earth. But Mama was a different kind of religious person. She wasn't the kind who just believed in praying and sitting down. She taught us: 'You pray—then you get up and go after it.'"

Medgar was, on the outside, an average child who pursued the normal interests of southern country boys—hunting small game such as squirrels and rabbits, fishing at the local stream, and, with Charles as the "promoter," getting into harmless fights with other boys.

But even though he was usually Charles' partner in "crime," Medgar was really a quiet and gentle child, loathing to slaughter hogs when it came time. He spent hours in solitary activities, such as reading or kicking a can down a long dirt road toward the woods. Like many bright children, Medgar dreamed of faraway worlds in which he could be a hero. The real world offered few such opportunities.

It could have been a typical rural southern childhood..., except for the fact that Medgar was a prisoner in the enemy camp, a black boy in a white man's world. It was not necessary for his

Medgar Evers with his mother and grandmother. The Everses were hardworking and always managed to make ends meet. They were justifiably proud of their self-sufficiency and were respected

in both the black and white communities. Father James and mother Jessie were strong people. A devout Christian, she insisted the Evers family attend church for four services a week.

parents to teach him that.

One day, Medgar and Charles were in the town square when Theodore G. Bilbo, a long-standing Mississippi politician, was making a speech. Bilbo was such an ardent segregationist that he advocated deporting all blacks to Africa.

On this day, Bilbo—at this time a U.S. Senator—was giving his usual pro-segregation spiel to an almost all-white audience. Almost, because Medgar and Charles were sitting at the edges of the crowd. Bilbo declared, "If we fail to hold high the wall of separation between the races, we will live to see that day when those two nigger boys right there will be asking for everything that is ours by right." And he pointed to the two Evers boys. The crowd turned around and stared at them. The boys knew what kind of attitude they were up against. But they also knew how to fight.

Jessie Evers urged her sons not to hate the whites, for hate was a poison that ate away at the heart. For any southern black, especially youngsters with an easily wounded sense of justice, this was an especially tough lesson to learn.

At first, Charles and Medgar channeled their anger into relatively harmless pranks. They would pick pecans, several bushels worth, for a white widow. This woman "paid" them with a small bucketful of pecans. Miffed at this meager return for a whole day's work, the Evers boys would return to the woman's barn and abduct the bushels of pecans they had picked that day. They'd take the stolen pecans to a white pecan-seller named McMillan.

McMillan paid three cents per bushel, but he often cheated the scales for blacks. So Charles and Medgar re-stole the pecans, put them in different sacks, and re-sold those same pecans to McMillan the next day. "We kept on doing this and found out that white folks are kinda dumb," Charles remembered.

Other times, their targets were white peddlers who drove into the black community to sell shoddy products at inflated prices. The boys would place boards with nails in them under the peddlers' trucks, and when they drove away or backed up—*speeewwwww*! went the tires. It looked just as funny as it sounded.

When the racists fought back, however, the laughter stopped. Medgar never forgot the lynching of one of his father's friends, Willie Tingle. Tingle had been accused of "leering"— looking in a sexually suggestive way—at a white woman. For that "crime," a mob dragged him by wagon through the main road in Decatur, right past the Evers house. They tied Tingle to a tree on the outskirts of town, and shot him dead. The lynchers left the dead man's bloody clothes near the tree, as a warning for other blacks not to get too "uppity."

This incident spelled out to Medgar in stark clarity that justice was different for white and for black people. The lynchers were never arrested, and no person dared protest, even when Tingle was dragged through the streets. Medgar was especially upset that no black people intervened. The paralysis of his people was the worst part of the lynching. He promised himself that, when he grew up, he would have a different reaction when trouble occurred.

But before he could fight injustice, Medgar had to go to school. James and Jessie Evers believed that an education would save their children from the drudgery that they had suffered. The Evers children, unlike their peers, were never taken out of school to work in the fields during harvest season.

The school for black children barely deserved the name. It was a small one-room building with a cracked roof, too cold in the winter and too hot in the spring. Up to one hundred children of various grades were crowded into the cramped room. To add insult to injury, the white children—who had a shiny yellow bus to take them to their school—would spit and throw rocks at the blacks when they passed in the road.

It was due to will and natural intelligence that Medgar gained enough knowledge under those circumstances to earn the right to go to high school. The nearest high school for blacks

Black churches in the South were not only a refuge in the years of persecution, they also provided the Christian values that came in the 1950s and 1960s to provide the basis for the Christian non-violent movement that would overturn segregation.

was miles away, but Medgar walked to get there. The thirst for knowledge had been awakened. He was optimistic that a better life was within reach, if he worked for it. Nothing the world threw at him from that point forward would change that view.

In 1940, Charles enlisted in the U.S. Army. At that time, the armed forces were segregated, and there were limits to how far a black could rise up in the ranks. That did not prevent young black men from enlisting in droves. Service paid twenty-one dollars a month at the time with free room and board.

Medgar, once again following his brother's example, dropped out of Newton High School to join the army. World War II had just started, and everyone was filled with patriotic fervor. Medgar's all-black unit saw action in France. But it would not be the new geographic vistas that would make the greatest impression on a teenage soldier. It was the revelation that the way whites and blacks related to each other in Mississippi was *not* instinctive.

Like many young men, Medgar had adopted the habit of using vulgar language, not because vulgarity was in his nature but because he wanted to be "one of the boys." But a white lieutenant pointed out to Medgar that intelligent people, such as Medgar, did not need to resort to low language. "You have a good vocabulary. You can

A Harper's Weekly cover for the Saturday, November 16, 1867, issue showing blacks voting. Former slaves were immediately given the right to vote following the Civil War.

say what you want without swearing every other word." Medgar never forgot what this lieutenant said and vowed to return to high school when his term of service was over.

Another shock was the French people's utter lack of racism. They treated blacks as soldiers, no more and no less. Medgar was even able to date a young French girl with no objection from her family—something that would have been unthinkable in the South.

Despite attempts by some white soldiers to poison the French minds against the blacks with outrageous tales, such as that blacks had monkey-like tails hidden in their pants, Medgar left the war with positive memories. He was determined to apply what he had learned in Europe at home.

World War II was a watershed event for black servicemen. They discovered the irony of fighting to liberate other nations while they were denied liberty in their own country. They were asked to assume the responsibilities of American citizenship without being granted many of the rights. The fuse of social revolution had been lit, and there was no turning back. Especially for Medgar Evers.

Shortly after his twenty-first birthday, Medgar, Charles, and four other blacks journeyed to the county clerk's office to register to vote. Although this was perfectly legal as far as written law was concerned, the unwritten, "real" law dictated otherwise.

The idea of blacks voting *en masse* was frightening to the segregationist power mavens. Blacks with ballots could easily deprive them of their jobs. Blacks could take over previously white-dominated power posts such as the county commissioners court, sheriffs' departments, and city offices. Some whites feared that once in power, blacks would reciprocate the treatment they received from white society. Whites would lose the scapegoat that made even the poorest and most ignorant of them feel superior.

After the Civil War, the United States government took over the defeated South and divided it into five military districts. For the first time, blacks were allowed to vote and 700,000 of them were registered by 1867. Almost all of them registered with the Republican party, the party of Lincoln. Blacks were elected to congress, to lieutenant governorships. But this new freedom did not last for long.

At Mississippi's Constitutional Convention of 1890, new voting laws were enacted. One was a literacy test, in which a prospective voter was required to be able to read and/or understand any section of the Mississippi Constitution. Another was a two-dollar poll tax—two dollars was not small change in 1890. Although these new rules disenfranchised some poor, illiterate whites, their primary purpose was to end the black vote. Indeed, the county circuit clerks were given discretionary power as to whom to accept and whom to reject. The U.S. Supreme Court allowed the new rules in 1898: "[The provisions] do not on their face discriminate between the races...." The last black Reconstruction congressman left office in 1901, and those particular doors were closed to blacks for decades.

Literacy tests and poll taxes were not the only ways to keep blacks away from the ballot box. Voting booths were placed far from black communities. Only whites were allowed to vote in primary elections. Black voters were faced with loss of jobs or mortgages. When all else failed, there was good old-fashioned intimidation. Bilbo said, "The best way to keep a nigger from the polls on election day is to visit him the night before."

The Evers house was visited—first by whites, then by blacks who wanted to avoid "trouble" in town. They all had the same message: "Don't show up to vote on election day." It was not necessary to spell out the consequences.

But the Evers boys and their friends would not be deterred. On election day, they met at the Evers house and trekked toward the courthouse, a group of young men who had fought for their country now going to exercise their right to vote.

No other blacks in Decatur dared appear in

public on that day. When the would-be voters arrived at the courthouse, a posse of armed white men greeted them. Some of these men had been their childhood playmates, the sons of their mothers' employers. Faced with this strong deterrent, the group retreated but was not defeated—not completely. "I made up my mind that it would not be like that again—at least not for me," Medgar said later. And it wasn't. The very next year, 1947, they did vote in the county election.

After this, Medgar returned to high school. He was one of the oldest in his class, but the desire to learn outweighed any embarrassment. The experience in the army and the attempt to vote raised his hopes that a better life for himself and his peers was within reach. For the first time, he really enjoyed and sought out knowledge. From his English teacher, Mrs. Johnson, he learned how to accumulate a tremendous vocabulary—one that would later send his friends running to the nearest dictionary. But he himself did not aspire to become a teacher, mainly because teaching was one of the few professions for blacks that whites approved of. He did not want white approval but white respect. And education, including a college degree, was the first step toward earning it.

Chapter Three

Education

WITH THE HELP OF his G.I. Bill and a football scholarship, Medgar Evers enrolled at Alcorn State University in the fall of 1948. Alcorn, located in a tree-rich area about forty miles south of Vicksburg, was one of Mississippi's two universities for blacks (Jackson State was the other). It was a hand-me-down school, having originally been built as a white military school until its "conversion" in 1871. The Mississippi Constitution of 1869 ordered public education for everyone, black and white. Although it was not yet officially mandated that blacks and whites attend

---

With the help of his G.I. Bill and a football scholarship, Medgar Evers was able to enroll at Alcorn State University, where Medgar came to full bloom and lettered in football and track.

Myrlie Beasley, the future wife of Medgar Evers, was a talented pianist and wanted to pursue a major in music but neither Alcorn nor Jackson State offered a music major at the time.

She applied for a grant to study music at an out-of-state college but was turned down when the black president of Jackson State declared his college offered "plenty of courses for musicians."

separate schools, Alcorn, a land-grant institution, was created as the black counterpart
to Mississippi State University. It was named
for James L. Alcorn, Mississippi's first
Republican governor. One of the most strik-
ing features of the campus was the chapel,
built without the use of nails by slaves.
(Actually, prior to the Civil War, the Alcorn
campus housed a private college for white
males, known as Oakland College.)

In the protected atmosphere of the all-black
colleges, there were opportunities for leadership and achievement that were not always
forthcoming in the "outside" world. Medgar
came into full bloom at Alcorn. He was a member of the debate team, the college choir, the
YMCA, and lettered in football and track. He
edited the campus newspaper and yearbook,
served as the class president in his junior
year, and, to top it all off, was chosen for list-
ing in the *Who's Who in American Colleges* for
1951–52.

Although it was certainly possible to obtain
a quality education at institutions like Alcorn,
they were still underfunded and lacked some
of the amenities that white students took for
granted. Myrlie Beasley, the future wife of
Medgar Evers, knew this firsthand. A talented pianist, Myrlie wanted to pursue a major
in music. But neither Alcorn nor Jackson

State offered a music major. The State of Mississippi offered, on paper, grants to black students to attend out-of-state colleges if they wanted to pursue a major unavailable at Alcorn or Jackson. This prevented blacks from attempting to enroll in the white colleges while paying lip service to the "separate but equal" decree of the Supreme Court.

Myrlie applied to the Board of Higher Learning for this grant, which required letters from the two black colleges confirming their lack of a music major. The black president of Jackson State declared that his college offered plenty of courses for musicians, and Myrlie's application was rejected. Perversely, the Board of Higher Learning made it all but impossible to receive this grant through tacitly influencing their employees, the black college presidents.

Medgar Evers' major was business administration, which fortunately *was* offered at Alcorn. This was his small rebellion against the teaching profession, but he doubtless was aware that there were few black businessmen in Mississippi at the time. Still, he bet on a future with more opportunities for blacks. His YMCA group met once a month with students at Millsaps College, a white school in Jackson, where the two groups debated world affairs. Evers knew that blacks could hold their own with whites. All they needed were more opportunities to do so.

His approach to college was nothing if not businesslike. Eschewing smoking, drinking, and fraternity shenanigans, he preferred to spend his spare time studying and earning money. For that, he gained the respect of the Alcorn community.

One person who felt more than respect was Myrlie Beasley, who knew right from the moment she met Medgar Evers that he was someone special. This happened in front of the college president's house, at a seemingly casual gathering of football players and freshman girls. Myrlie at first mistook his name as "Edgar Evans," but there was no mistaking the impression he made on her. "There was something in the way he spoke, the way he carried himself, in his politeness, that made him stand out even from the others I met that day," Myrlie said in her autobiography.

This was exactly what Myrlie's grandmother and aunt had warned her against. Like other young ladies reared in similar households, the Vicksburg native had been schooled about the dangers of m-e-n. Specifically, those "worldly veterans" who would line up for the possibility to "use" her—leaving Myrlie to wonder exactly what was meant by "use." In 1950, Myrlie was a seventeen-year-old fresh-

Y ON THE CAMPUS

ASSOCIATION WORK

While at Alcorn, Medgar Evers met white college students at Millsaps through a program of the Student YMCA-YWCA, which for many years had provided the only means for young southern whites and blacks to become acquainted and seek understanding.

man. Medgar Evers was twenty-five, "older" by the standards of the time.

Medgar soon took to passing by the music studio where Myrlie practiced piano. At first he told her it was because he liked the music. That was only a pretense; he was no fan of classical music and wanted an excuse to see her.

They began to date regularly, and Myrlie noticed that Medgar was not one for open affection. He told her that his actions would convey all that she needed to know about his feelings, and also that he would never declare love unless he really meant it. He was also not forthcoming with his money, but that was more due to his responsible attitude toward life than to stinginess.

Despite his reputation for dating many girls, Medgar had firm standards for anyone who wished to become his wife. She had to be intelligent, friendly, neat, and fond of children—and had to devote herself to him wholeheartedly. Myrlie qualified on all of these counts, but made it a point to go out with other boys when he dated other girls. He secretly respected that.

Summers for Medgar Evers were no time for idleness. He and brother Charles, also a student at Alcorn, would get into their car and drive over seven hundred miles to Chicago,

Medgar and Myrlie Evers. When they met Myrlie was a seven-teen year old and Medgar was twenty-five, an "older" man by the standards of the time. He pretended to like classical music but that was only an excuse to visit Myrlie while she practiced.

Illinois, where they stayed with their half-sister Eva. While this drive was no joyride—the car was rusty and recalcitrant, and the brothers were forbidden, while in the South, to use the restrooms at white-owned service stations—the extra money they made in Chicago made the trip worthwhile. Medgar and Charles worked at jobs involving manual labor, such as construction and meat-packing.

Much of the money earned in Chicago made its way back to Decatur, and James and Jessie Evers made some major revisions to their house. Now it had four bedrooms, a gas heater, and indoor plumbing at last. Medgar and Charles were doubtless happy to help give their parents the home that they deserved after years of hard, selfless work.

Eva lived in Chicago's South Side, which was by now firmly entrenched as the "Negro" side of town. Almost every northern and midwestern city had its black ghetto.

In 1860, right before the Civil War, ninety-five percent of U.S. blacks lived in the South. A century later, only fifty-four percent did so. The remainder were mostly concentrated in the northeast and central states. Especially after 1910, the black migration steadily increased, except for a lull during the Great Depression of the 1930s. Economic factors were the major reason for this phenomenon.

Charles Evers, Medgar's brother, was also a student at Alcorn. Come summer, they would drive over seven hundred miles to Chicago to find jobs in construction or at meat packing plants.

A boll weevil epidemic (which damaged cotton fields) and a severe drought in 1916-1917 reduced the number of menial agricultural jobs available; northern industry, needing new workers, actively recruited southern blacks as well as poor whites. Testimonials from those blacks who had moved north and upbeat advertising in the black press also increased migration.

When southern blacks moved to northern cities, they clustered together in communities like Chicago's South Side or New York's Harlem. This was not because blacks preferred segregation, as some pundits claimed, but because of the natural tendency of migrant ethnic groups to live close to friends and others of like background.

But unlike European immigrants, blacks could not hide their ethnicity with pseudonyms and affected accents. Consequently, the usual roads out of the ghettos—education, entrepreneurship, initiative—were all but closed to them. Racism was not institutionalized as it was in the South, but it existed, like a lingering bad odor. Blacks could share schools, beaches, theaters, buses, and libraries with whites, but they could not share lives.

Medgar Evers was used to racism, but what he really hated about Chicago—especially that South Side—was its dirtiness, its black-on-black crime, and its lack of free, open spaces like he had known in Decatur. Chicago had higher wages and greater personal freedom, but that was not enough to encourage him to live there. What he wanted to do was bring the mobility that blacks enjoyed up North down to Mississippi.

One of his pastimes in Chicago was driving through the rapidly growing, nearly all-white suburb of Evanston. He was impressed with the cleanliness, peace, and beauty of this enclave. This was the America of advertisements and motion pictures—two places, besides suburbs, where black faces were not common. Still, he took Myrlie to Evanston and asked, hopefully, if this would not be a wonderful place to raise children.

Myrlie, too, was in Chicago during the summer of 1951. She knew that three whole months without Medgar would be miserable, so she plotted to find work in Chicago. Fortunately she had an aunt living there, so there was a ready-made chaperone to appease her grandmother. Although most of their time that summer was spent working, Medgar and Myrlie found time on the weekends to be together. They took full advantage of nonsegregated Chicago. Myrlie had never learned to swim because there were no swimming pools for blacks in Vicksburg. Medgar, tried, unsuccessfully, to teach her to swim at the beach. She became furious at him, but it soon became just another reason to kiss and make up.

Myrlie came to dislike Chicago, too, and for more reasons than crime and dirt. The big city was not conducive to the friendliness and concern seen among the citizens of rural burgs. "Millions of people lived in Chicago," she said, "but it was no one's home town."

The summer did have one positive event: the couple started to talk about marriage. But they wondered how soon it could happen. Medgar's G. I. Bill and football scholarship were about to expire, and there was a strong likelihood that he would have to dedicate his savings to finish school. Myrlie wondered what would happen to her own scholarship if she married. Without it, her college career would be over.

One August evening, Medgar appeared at Myrlie's door with a shocking message: he was considering putting an end to the relationship. He said that she was probably too young to think about marriage, that perhaps it was better for her if she dated others before taking this major step. He thought that he was doing the right thing.

Instead of breaking into tears, Myrlie became angry. She did not see concern in his attitude, only self-interest. "Why don't you ask me if I feel ready to settle down?" she asked.

When he did, she told him that he had all of the qualities that she wanted in a husband, and she felt no need to look further. If he himself was not ready for marriage, she said, he should have told her that instead of hiding behind the pretense of thinking about her feelings.

Instead of walking away or pleading his case, Medgar had a surprise for Myrlie—a box containing an engagement ring. The diamond ring was modest in size, but "along with it goes all the love I have," he said.

Myrlie did not know what to say. A moment before, she had been infuriated with him. Now, she knew she would be his for life.

But, as it was for many young couples considering marriage, the problem of money loomed like a black cloud. They could not survive on Medgar's income alone (besides his G.I. Bill, he worked as a courier for a dry cleaner near Alcorn), so Myrlie took up typing for hire. They wanted to live in Vet City, an off-campus housing development for married couples, but would have to share an apartment with another couple to do so.

At least the cost of the wedding itself was taken care of. Myrlie's grandmother took a long time to come around, but her aunt was more supportive and agreed to pay for a church wedding, which took place in Vicksburg on Christmas Eve 1951.

After a brief, low-cost honeymoon spent visiting each other's in-laws, the Everses returned to school after New Year's Day. They discovered that they would have to wait at least a month before moving into Vet City, so they returned to their separate dorms. It may seem hard to believe today, but even though Medgar and Myrlie were now married they were restricted, because Myrlie was a sophomore, to two dates a week. They circumvented that rule by spending time studying together. Both Medgar and Myrlie were determined to keep their grades up, to prove to themselves and their families—and especially Myrlie's grandmother—that marriage would not prevent them from graduating from Alcorn.

Near the end of his senior year, Medgar was interviewed by the Magnolia Mutual Insurance Company, a recently-created business owned by Mississippi blacks. Medgar saw this as an excellent opportunity to begin his post-college business career *and* remain in Mississippi. Myrlie, however, was not pleased with this idea. As far as she was concerned, Mississippi was *not* the place for an intelligent, ambitious black man to make his dreams come true. Chicago, however cold and grimy it was, was more hospitable to blacks.

But when Medgar's application for employment was approved, Myrlie accepted their fate. She remembered the many arguments she had with her grandmother regarding Medgar, and she was going to stand by him, no matter what.

After Medgar's graduation in 1952, it was off to Mound Bayou, an all-black community in the Mississippi Delta where the insurance company was based. Medgar thought he was about to become a serious wage-earner. Instead, he found his true calling.

Chapter Four

A Family Man

MAGNOLIA MUTUAL Insurance Company was the brainchild of Dr. Theodore R. M. Howard, aided by a group of black businessmen. Dr. Howard, a former trainee at the Mayo Clinic, was appointed chief surgeon at Mound Bayou's Taborian Hospital in 1942. He developed it into the state's largest hospital for blacks, with seventy-six beds and two operating rooms. Here, black patients were guaranteed quality care in clean facilities and did not have to bring their own sheets and eating utensils as they did in segregated hospitals. Dr. Howard was beloved by the Mound Bayou

The Mississippi Delta. When Medgar Evers finished college at Alcorn State, he moved to all-black Mound Bayou to sell insurance, although he made little more money than in college.

community and respected even by his white planter neighbors. Dr. Howard's good reputation no doubt convinced Medgar Evers that Magnolia Mutual was *the* place to work.

In 1952, Mound Bayou had a population of only 1,328, all black. It was a sleepy, drab town with almost nothing in the way of special interest or entertainment. It was no place for an optimistic young wife like Myrlie Evers.

Myrlie worked at the insurance company's Mound Bayou headquarters as a typist, and her days usually consisted of working, then going back to the couple's two-room apartment and waiting for Medgar to come home, which frequently didn't happen until late in the evening.

At least Medgar's job took him outdoors. He was assigned as his "territory" the town of Clarksdale, and he would drive about twenty-five miles to and from that town each day. He went door-to-door selling insurance to the black residents. Because most of them were farmers, they might work until late at night, and Medgar would have to wait for them.

His notions of quick prosperity through hard work disappeared. His income was just a tiny improvement over that in his last year of college. He had to borrow money to buy a car, a refrigerator, and furniture. But his income was not his biggest problem.

All around Mound Bayou was the Mississippi Delta, the throne of "King Cotton." Its generous topsoil and muggy weather brought riches to the white planters—and misery to black laborers.

In 1954, the U.S. Department of Agriculture paid $2,000,000 to the richest Mississippi cotton growers for their surplus. What many people who dressed themselves in Mississippi cotton did not know or care about—and those who did know were not inclined to talk much about it—was the human cost of that cotton.

After the abolition of slavery, the southern landowners needed another means to keep cheap labor in the fields, so they devised the system of "sharecropping," which in concept appeared to be a fair deal.

Sharecropping was the trading of labor for sustenance. A family—most commonly a black family—would occupy a house and small plot of land rent-free. In return, they would agree to help work the planter's other land and to give the planter a percentage of the crop they raised on the land they occupied.

On the surface, this appeared to be a fair exchange. However, in practice, landowners were able to take advantage of the sharecroppers through a variety of abuses, keeping them in a form of peonage not much different from slavery.

One of the most serious abuses occurred with the "furnish," or line of credit the landowner gave to the sharecropper to buy food, seed, and other supplies, which had to be purchased at the nearby general store—which the planter usually owned himself. Often, the planter would jack up the prices at the store, forcing the sharecropper to dig deeper into credit—and debt.

The planter could—and would—"fix" his account books so that he could "prove" that the sharecropper was still in debt at season's end. Many sharecroppers were illiterate and therefore unable to prove the planter wrong; others were intimidated into asking no questions. Those who did attempt to fight the chicanery found that the law was not on their side. A black sharecropper could not win in court against a white property owner—especially in the Mississippi Delta.

If a sharecropper tried to flee before his debt was paid, the force of law would drag him right back.

There was little gain for the pain. Earning $3.50 a day or *less*, the average sharecropper's yearly income hovered at $1200. That was shockingly low even in the early 1950s. The Everses, poor as they were, earned at least twice that.

On his rounds, Medgar would visit "homes"

where the twentieth century had not yet reached: shacks without windows, doors, or even a floor to stand on; no electricity, plumbing, or stoves; barefoot children in ragged clothes, who were not washed and whose hair was allowed to grow into a mass of impossible tangles. These children were invariably under-educated, because the black schools operated according to the cotton-planting schedule. During the peak planting and harvesting season of early spring until late fall, the schools were closed so that the children could work in the fields—to increase the planter's profit, of course.

At first, Medgar was upset with the sharecroppers themselves for giving in to their desperate conditions without a fight. He thought about how he had been reared with pride and self-respect despite the poverty. His own parents wouldn't think of taking their children out of school to work for a white man. But as he learned more about the sharecroppers' special circumstances, he understood that their hopelessness was more enforced from without than bred from within.

Medgar would take these people clothing and other necessities, but he knew that they needed much more. He felt not only helpless but guilty about attempting to sell them insurance they could barely afford. But he

After college, Medgar Evers moved to the all black town of Mound Bayou in the Mississippi Delta to sell insurance. Most of his clients were sharecroppers, trading labor for sustenance. A family would occupy a house and a small plot of land rent free.

In return they worked the owner's land for a percentage of the crop they raised. On the surface it appeared to be fair. However, landowners were able to take advantage of the system through a variety of abuses. Above is a typical sharecropper's cabin.

knew too that if he didn't sell it to them, a white salesman would, and a white salesman was more likely to cheat them or treat them unfairly.

The sharecroppers' plight dominated Medgar's thoughts and words, much to Myrlie's dismay. Not that she was insensitive to suffering, but she had her own problems and worries at home. How would she and Medgar be able to start a family on their meager income? Why did the sharecropper problem take him away from her even when they were together? This was not how she imagined married life would be.

Medgar decided that the Delta was the ideal place to organize new chapters of the National Association for the Advancement of Colored People. He probably learned about the organization in a small paperbound textbook used in Mississippi black schools, which was "sneaked in" by black teachers who wished to present an alternative to the state-sanctioned textbooks that painted a glowing picture of slavery and segregation.

Although the NAACP had been founded in 1909, it was slow to spread through Mississippi. The NAACP had been present in Mississippi since the late 1910s, but it had no state conference until 1945, and still had only a handful of chapters in the state. Medgar realized that the NAACP would give Delta blacks a sense of empowerment, a belief that they could do something to help themselves and influence their government.

In the summer of 1952, the Regional Council of Negro Leadership—of which Dr. Howard was a prominent member—held its first annual meeting in Mound Bayou. The guest speaker of the meeting was Thurgood Marshall, a lawyer for the NAACP (who would become the first black justice of the U.S. Supreme Court). The meeting was held in a huge tent, just like an old-time prayer meeting.

Medgar informed all of his Delta customers about the meeting and urged them to attend. Some did, but many more stayed home. Those who attended were brave, for landowners were not above seeking retribution against sharecroppers who did anything that could be interpreted as hostile to white interests. Even sporting a bumper sticker printed by the Regional Council that read, "DON'T BUY GAS WHERE YOU CAN'T USE THE RESTROOM," was risky.

Around this time, the unintentionally neglected Myrlie discovered that she was pregnant. She had suffered a miscarriage before, so Medgar made an effort to spend more time with her. Still, the prospect of

The historic Supreme Court Decision of 1954 in Brown v. Board of Education of Topeka *was the result of many years of effort by a staff of lawyers from the NAACP, who pursued several cases*

from the lower courts, appealing the policy of "separate but equal," until it was overturned. Above, Thurgood Marshall, Donald Gaines Murrey, and Charles Houston, work on the case.

bringing a new black person into the world made him even more determined to help make that world a more just one.

Medgar became fascinated with the Mau Mau uprising in Kenya, a country in eastern Africa. Kenya had been an English colony since 1895, and many Europeans settled in the Kenyan highlands—forcing the black natives, called Kikuyu, off the land. The Kikuyu formed a secret guerrilla army, the Mau Mau, to scare the whites out of Kenya and reclaim their country. Their leader was Jomo Kenyatta, a black man who spoke and dressed like a European but had dedicated his life to empowering African people.

The white southern press painted a picture of the Mau Maus as savages, but in reality the word "savage" was more appropriate to describe the Kenyan police, who had killed about eight thousand Mau Maus while only seventy whites had been killed during the uprising.

Medgar wondered if the Mau Mau idea would work in Mississippi. That would turn the weapon of clandestine terrorism right back at white vigilantes. He was by no means a violent man, but the physical and psychological violence against Mississippi blacks could no longer go on without a response.

At the same time, he started to read the

Bible that he and Myrlie had received as a wedding present. His mother's strong religious beliefs had not been passed down to him, and he did not attend church, but he was searching for an antidote to the violent thoughts that he knew in his heart were no real solution.

Eventually, he abandoned the idea of a Mississippi Mau Mau army, although that movement had been successful in Kenya. But he did say to Myrlie that if their baby was born a boy, he would be named Kenyatta. But "Kenyatta Evers" was just a bit *too* unusual for 1953, so when their expected son was born in June of that year, Myrlie placed "Darrell" in front of it. That suited Medgar just fine.

When Myrlie was forced to return to work, she had no choice but to send little Darrell to her grandmother's house in Vicksburg for three-and-a-half months until she could hire a suitable baby-sitter. Middle- and upper-class women, mostly white, had the luxury of staying home with their children, but many black families needed two incomes just to survive.

Medgar's efforts to enlist more members of the NAACP were beginning to succeed, even in the Delta. The first community to become eligible for its own branch from his efforts— a branch required at least fifty members—was Shelby, and more were to follow. By late 1953, there were twenty-one NAACP branches in Mississippi, with sixteen hundred members total. That may seem a small number considering that Mississippi's black population was more than one million, but with the state's history of racist terrorism, it was a promising start.

Myrlie was pleased that Medgar had succeeded in an endeavor he believed in and thought that now he would turn more attention to Darrell and herself. But at an NAACP meeting in Mound Bayou, he showed that his activism had only begun.

At that meeting, Dr. E.J. Stringer, then the Mississippi state president of the NAACP, suggested that now was the time to desegregate the University of Mississippi. Only recently had the NAACP switched its party line from condoning "separate but equal" (with the emphasis on *equal*) to taking a firm stand against segregation.

The term "separate but equal" came from the *Plessy v. Ferguson* case in 1898, in which a black man, Homer Plessy, sued the New Orleans government after being arrested for riding in a railroad car reserved for whites only. Plessy's case made it all the way to the Supreme Court, where it was decided that segregation, as long as whites and blacks had facilities of equal quality, was not an "unreasonable" use of the states' powers. The court's decision was that the Fourteenth Amendment to the U.S. Constitution, which granted full citizenship rights to ex-slaves, was not meant to "enforce social as distinguished from political...equality, or a co-mingling of the two races upon terms unsatisfactory to each other."

The concept of "separate but equal" never worked in the real world. In practice, governments cared little about ensuring that black facilities, especially schools and colleges, were on par with those for whites.

Some colleges in other southern states, however, had been successfully desegregated at the graduate school level, with help from the NAACP's lawyers, who pursued cases all the way up to the Supreme Court. What Dr. Stringer wanted to know at the Mound Bayou meeting was who would be willing to take on the toughest challenge, Ole Miss?

Chapter Five

A Plea for Law

EVERS STOOD UP at the meeting and announced his intention to apply to the University of Mississippi law school. As a lawyer, he said, he could best help his people. His announcement was greeted with delighted applause—a response he would not get at home.

When he told Myrlie the news, her reaction was not one of pride. It was shock and horror—and not because the idea was dangerous. Myrlie's concerns were more practical: how would Medgar find the time or money to go to law school? If he was accepted, he would have to give up his job at the insurance company. The

At an NAACP meeting in Mound Bayou in late 1953, Medgar Evers announced his plans to enroll at the University of Mississippi (Ole Miss) law school. He was rejected.

family was barely surviving, even with the two of them working. Especially with a new baby in the house, it was hardly the best time to think about law school.

Medgar's answer to that was that sacrifices were necessary to make progress, and that someone had to be the first to try to desegregate Ole Miss and it might as well be him. He would borrow and save whatever was necessary, but this project could not wait. He was doing this to open the door for his children and for all black children to attend Ole Miss or any college of their choice, in whatever major they wanted. The more educated blacks became, he knew, the less likely they would be to accept subhuman conditions, and the more determined they would be to demand their rights.

When Evers requested that his Alcorn College transcripts be sent to the University of Mississippi law school and filled out his application, he became statewide news. The Jackson *Daily News* spelled it out in big, bold letters on January 22, 1954: NEGRO APPLIES TO ENTER OLE MISS. The public life of Medgar Evers had begun—and anyone who wanted to stop him from going to Ole Miss knew his name.

When Myrlie raised the possibility of danger on campus, Medgar replied that blacks in Mississippi were *always* in danger, even if only of starving to death. Nothing she could say

Medgar Evers, at about the time he applied to the University of Mississippi School of Law. On rejecting Evers, the attorney general ruled that, henceforth, all applicants had to have references from five alumni of the Ole Miss School of Law.

would convince him that he was doing the wrong thing.

Dr. E. R. Jobe, executive secretary of the State Board of Trustees of Institutions of Higher Learning, said that the board must receive word from Mississippi Attorney General James P. Coleman—a man who, as governor, would declare that blacks were not fit to vote—before considering the application. Evers had applied for the fall 1954 term.

In the meantime, Myrlie discovered that she was pregnant again. She believed that this was an excellent reason for Medgar to give up his crazy idea of applying to Ole Miss law school. But to him this was only another reason to go ahead.

Even Medgar's parents were unhappy about his plans. James believed that it was unfair for Medgar to make Myrlie and the children suffer, and he said so in no uncertain terms during a family visit to Decatur. Medgar was upset by his father's reaction, but what could he do?

Tragically, Mr. Evers did not have much longer to live. He became seriously ill and was admitted to a hospital in Union, Mississippi. When Medgar rushed to the scene, he found his father in the hospital basement, the designated area for blacks. It was hardly the most dignified place to die.

At the same time, another black man lay

injured in the basement, having been shot in the leg during an altercation with a policeman. An angry swarm of white faces crowded at the windows, seemingly poised to break in and drag the injured man away at any moment.

Even in death or injury, a black man in Mississippi could not escape the scourge of racism.

While Evers waited for word to come from Attorney General Coleman, good things were happening in faraway Washington, D.C.

About three years before, a black man named Oliver Brown had sued the Board of Education of Topeka, Kansas, because his daughter was not allowed to attend an all-white elementary school five blocks from their home; the nearest black school was four times the distance away. Although Topeka's high schools were integrated, state law permitted but did not mandate segregation in elementary schools in cities with populations larger than fifteen thousand.

A federal court in Topeka held that black and white schools were substantially equal, and thus did not violate the *Plessy v. Ferguson* decision. Brown took his case to the U.S. Supreme Court, and his case was judged along with other school segregation cases from Delaware, South Carolina, and Virginia.

All of these cases pointed to the Fourteenth Amendment to the Constitution, which required equal protection under the law. It took three years of sifting through constitutional, sociological, and historical issues to reach a verdict, but at last, on May 17, 1954, the Court declared that school segregation was indeed a violation of the Fourteenth Amendment and therefore illegal under the Constitution.

Chief Justice Earl Warren asked, "Does segregation of children in public schools solely on the basis of race, even though the facilities be equal, deprive children of the minority group of educational opportunity?" The answer was yes, because segregation itself was antithetical to a democratic society. Furthermore, modern times could not be compared to the nineteenth century, when *Plessy v. Ferguson* was decided. The Constitution was meant to evolve with current knowledge.

The ruling shook the soul of the South. Many southern governors declared that they would uphold the law of the land, as they had vowed to do when they were inaugurated. But others, especially in Mississippi, were not as accepting. The Jackson *Clarion-Ledger* called May 17 "a black day of tragedy for the South." Senator James O. Eastland, who upheld the grand old tradition of Theodore Bilbo, condemned the Supreme Court for its "disregard of its oath and duty."

Whites all across Mississippi feared the impli-

Earl Warren was chief justice of the U.S. Supreme Court when it made the historic 1954 decision requiring desegregation of public schools, and he wrote the Court's opinion.

cations of the ruling—and what is racism but a manifestation of fear of the unknown? It was one thing for their children to play with the children of their servants. It was quite another for their children to attend the same school as the children of their servants. Some paranoid minds thought that school desegregation would inevitably lead to (shudder) *marriage between the races* and the end of "decent" southern civilization.

Thus were born the White Citizens' Councils, supposedly the brainchild of one Robert "Tut" Patterson, a Delta planter whose hobby was writing racist and anti-Semitic pamphlets. The initial goal of these councils was to make blacks suffer economically. They believed—with good reason—that if the wolf was planted firmly at the door of black people, they would be too preoccupied to worry about political or social equality.

Blacks, of course, felt differently about the *Brown* decision. Finally, a court—the most influential court in America—had said that state-sanctioned segregation was inexcusably wrong. They had a sense that, after centuries of oppression in America, a change was coming, and coming soon. Medgar Evers was happy, too. He felt that this would make it much easier to get into the University of Mississippi.

The governor of Mississippi at that time,

Robert "Tut" Patterson was one of the main leaders of the opposition to desegregation, founding the White Citizens' Councils which promoted the philosophy of "white supremacy."

Hugh White, tried to get around the Supreme Court ruling in a "reasonable" manner by gathering about a hundred black leaders in Jackson in July 1954 and making a pledge to spend millions to "equalize" black schools and thereby eliminate the need for desegregation. With that tempting bait, White believed, the black leaders would certainly agree to continue segregation voluntarily, and if they approved, the rest of Mississippi's blacks would approve as well.

These black leaders surprised White, however, by speaking out against the status quo. No amount of money in the world could make up for institutionalized racism. The Reverend H. H. Humes, a conservative black and one of White's closest allies, said, "you all should not be mad at us. Those were *white* men that rendered that decision. Not one colored man had anything to do with it."

All but one of these leaders signed a statement opposing efforts by white or black Mississippians to circumvent the *Brown* decision. An embittered White said, "You can't put faith in any of them [blacks]," but this was a major victory for the blacks who attended. They had not only spoken out in public, but they did it right to the governor's face.

In August 1954, Evers, accompanied by Dr. Jobe and A. P. Tureaud, an NAACP lawyer, went to Jackson for his interview with Attorney

General Coleman. Coleman questioned the sincerity of Evers' application. Was this just a publicity stunt? After all, Evers was twenty-nine (although he had earned his bachelor's degree only two years before) and had taken no law classes at Alcorn (there were none). And why would he not accept an out-of-state scholarship if he wanted so badly to go to law school?

Evers replied that it was only proper that he should study law in the state where he intended to practice.

Then Coleman asked if Evers actually planned to live and eat on the campus. Evers replied affirmatively and gave assurance that "I bathe regularly..., I wear clean clothes, and none of the brown of my skin will rub off. I won't contaminate the dormitory or the food."

When he returned to Mound Bayou, neighbors and friends warned him and Myrlie to "look out for strangers." Neither of them made a major deal over this; blacks who were thought to be "uppity" had to be extra-careful in Mississippi. But the Everses did not realize that this was only the beginning of a life under threat, a way of life that would not end until Medgar's death nine years later.

In September 1954, the household was blessed with another child, a daughter named Rena. Three days later, the Board of Higher Learning announced that Evers' application to Ole Miss had been rejected. He had done everything required, including sending in letters of recommendation from prominent citizens in his county—including some of his mother's former employers. But, said the board, Evers had to have sent in letters from Bolivar County, where Mound Bayou was located, and not Newton County, where his hometown of Decatur was. That was a little detail the board had not told him *before* he sent in his application.

To rub salt in the wound, the board also announced that from now on all applicants to the University of Mississippi law school had to obtain character references from five alumni of the school. Since all alumni were, of course, white, it was next to impossible for a black to fulfill this requirement. Ole Miss graduates and black people did not run in the same social circles.

But when one door closes, another opens. The NAACP was impressed with Evers' courage in applying to Ole Miss and with his work in recruiting new members—so impressed that it offered him the newly-created job of state field secretary for Mississippi—that is, the national office's head representative in Mississippi.

The NAACP, born in 1909 through the efforts of black and white activists such as W.E.B. Du Bois, Mary White Ovington, and Oswald Garrison Villard, had been one of a black per-

Under the system of "separate but equal," blacks and whites had separate facilities, not only schools but drinking fountains and waiting rooms in train and bus stations, as seen above. Although separate, they never managed to be equal.

son's best friends from its inception. After World
War II, however, it took on a more aggressive
role, from protecting the rights of blacks within
the law to trying to change the laws themselves.
The NAACP took advantage of U.S. courts,
which were slowly but surely becoming more
receptive to civil rights concerns.

Evers' new job was to investigate racial
harassment in Mississippi—of which there was
definitely no shortage—and especially the activities of the White Citizens' Councils, which were
stepping up their economic intimidation. People
who volunteered to work for the NAACP would
"mysteriously" lose their jobs or be turned down
for bank loans, or even receive unexpected tax
audits. One of the most ridiculous examples of
harassment was when Dr. Howard, who had
attended Governor White's get-together, was
ordered by the draft board to explain why he
should not be classified 1-A, or first in priority.
At that time, Dr. Howard was forty-seven years
old. Many employers, bank officers, and federal
agents in Mississippi were also members of
White Citizens' Councils.

A black man who owned seventy-three acres
of Delta farmland and a seven-room house was
not able to obtain federal loans to help run his
farm because he hosted a meeting of NAACP
members. This and many other affidavits, mostly gathered by Evers, were sent to the Eisen-

Medgar Evers worked not only regular business hours as Mississippi field secretary for the NAACP, but he spent many evenings conducting civil rights meeting such as the one above.

hower White House—where they were ignored.

To help people beset with financial problems, the NAACP contributed funds to the Tri-State Bank of Memphis, a black-owned bank, so that blacks in Mississippi could receive emergency loans when needed. This was yet another example of the NAACP coming to the rescue when "official" government was indifferent.

Evers gave notice to Dr. Howard at the Magnolia Mutual Insurance Company, and although Dr. Howard was unhappy to lose a valuable employee, he was also proud that Evers was moving on to a much more important job. At an orientation meeting in New York, Evers met other NAACP field secretaries from other states, who were busy with the agenda he had dreamed of while working among the sharecroppers. He saw just how big the NAACP was, solving problems all around the country—and he couldn't wait to get to work in Mississippi.

He discovered that he would be working in Jackson, the state capital, which necessitated a move from Mound Bayou. Myrlie was pleased with that prospect. Better yet, Medgar had also secured a job for her as his personal secretary. Now, she believed, they would spend much more time together. With their NAACP salaries bringing in $6500 a year, the Everses could afford a two-bedroom apartment and had room for Myrlie's grandmother to live with them and watch over Darrell and Rena during working hours.

The NAACP office in Jackson opened on January 23, 1955, and Gloster Current, the director of all NAACP branches and one of the Everses' personal friends, made a speech that in essence delineated the goal in Mississippi. "The NAACP will not rest," he said, "until every Negro in Mississippi who is eligible is granted the right of the ballot." Voting was real power; cities and counties with black majorities could conceivably put hard-line racist lawmakers out of their jobs.

At the Jackson office—where they were, for now, the only two occupants—Medgar made it clear to Myrlie that marriage was marriage, but business was business, and that while they were in the office they were to behave strictly as businesspeople. He even insisted that they call each other Mr. and Mrs. Evers while at work—to the amusement of visitors who came into the office.

Outside the office, however, Medgar was more gregarious. He made it a point to chat with strangers on the street, like a cheerful salesman. He thought that people would be less afraid of the NAACP if it had a smiling face—but he soon discovered that this would not be enough.

Chapter Six

Opposition to the Dream

IT IS IMPORTANT to remember that not all of the people who wanted to subvert the efforts of Medgar Evers and the NAACP were white.

Many blacks in so-called "leadership" positions were nothing more than mouthpieces for the white power structure. These were the black college presidents, ministers, planters, and government agents who had been given pieces of the American Dream in exchange for unwavering support (or at least a show of it) for the "way things were." Some of these even spied upon their fellow blacks and reported suspicious activities to police and sheriff's departments.

Medgar Evers endured increasing numbers of death threats and continued to work patiently but persistently for what he believed in, determined that life would be better for his children.

Why would a black person favor segregation? Many had known no other way of life and sincerely believed that it was the natural and correct order of things. Like white racists, they too were afraid of change. Some wanted nothing whatsoever to do with white people: experience had taught them that whites were good for nothing but creating misery.

In the case of public schools, some feared that the states would dismantle all public education for blacks before integrating all-white schools. Black teachers feared direct competition with white ones, because then the inferiority of the black teachers' training would be exposed and they would lose their jobs.

Percy Greene, a black editor of the Jackson *Advocate*, wrote an editorial that criticized Medgar Evers and praised Governor White's school equalization program. Greene made the unsubstantiated claim that eighty-five percent of Mississippi blacks disapproved of the *Brown* decision, and even said that "the NAACP is an enemy of the Negro race." Moreover, Greene did *not* point out that the money earmarked by White would go only to improving school *buildings*, not the teachers, textbooks, or equipment within those buildings. And the plan would not prevent *local* governments from underspending on black eduction. Yazoo County, located in the Delta, spent $245.55 per school year on each white child—while only $2.92 was spent for each black child.

The white press gleefully pounded on Greene's editorial as "evidence" that most blacks preferred segregation. One paper even called it "The Voice of A Negro." That was true—it was the voice of *a* Negro, not all.

To be fair, many of these "good Negroes" were motivated by self-preservation, just like German civilians who knew or guessed at the atrocities of the Holocaust but remained silent. To protest could mean loss of income, ostracism in the community—and even death.

In May 1955, the Supreme Court answered the question of when the states were to desegregate schools: "with all deliberate speed."

Mississippi's answer to that was a thumbed nose. The Jackson *Daily News* brazenly declared in an editorial, "YES, WE DEFY THE LAW." This was not America, they opined, this was *Mississippi*. And Mississippi would fight tooth and nail to preserve its way of life.

Medgar Evers took advantage of this new Supreme Court decision to encourage black parents at NAACP branch meetings throughout the state to petition for an immediate end to segregated schools. In Yazoo City, fifty-three people did so. What happened to them was typical of what happened to others who dared sign anti-segregation petitions.

As the southern states began to realize that their concept of "separate but equal" was being challenged because of the inequality of the facilities, they began to attempt to improve

the facilities, building new schools for blacks, such as the one above in Mississippi in the early 1960s. However, it was too late, for separation itself was seen as inherently unequal.

The Yazoo *Herald* ran a paid advertisement—likely bought by a White Citizens' Council—which listed the names, addresses, and phone numbers of those who had signed the petition. Carpenters, plumbers, and merchants saw their businesses evaporate. Stores would even refuse the money of petition-signers. Even when people took their names off the petition, the harassment continued.

Eventually, fifty-one of the fifty-three signatures were removed from the petition in Yazoo City—and the two names left had moved out of town.

As people lost their jobs and incomes, the Everses' office in Jackson was besieged with calls for help. Medgar urged petitioners to hang tough, but the promise of social gains tomorrow paled in comparison to hunger today. So he distributed food and clothing to those in need, and even allowed those who had been threatened with death to stay at his apartment. Myrlie said that his job was like "tending a caldron that could explode at any moment and often did and then exploded again before the fire from the last explosion had been extinguished."

Medgar had believed that hard work and persistence could move mountains; now he became frustrated at what he could *not* do. He might offer encouragement to the distressed, but he could not influence the *real* troublemakers.

Still, he could not and would not abandon the people who were counting on "Mr. Evers" to help them. What they needed most, even more than material sustenance, was hope. But soon, a tragedy would occur that would challenge even Medgar Evers' optimism.

One of Evers' colleagues was the Reverend George Lee, who worked at the Belzoni, Mississippi, branch of the NAACP. Reverend Lee was a Baptist minister, a store owner—and a registered voter. When he tried to vote, however, the county sheriff, Ike Shelton, simply refused to accept Lee's poll-tax payment. Lee reported Shelton's refusal to federal authorities, and Shelton quickly agreed to accept poll taxes from registered blacks from then on. Unfortunately, the story did not end there.

On May 7, 1955, Lee received an anonymous threat of death if he did not take his name off the voting rolls. Lee shrugged it off, but that night, as he was driving through the black section of town, he was shot in the face. He lost control of his car and ran into a house. Lee managed to get out of his car with part of his face blown away, but he died on the way to the hospital.

Evers was telephoned about an hour after Lee's death. He and Dr. A. H. McCoy, now the Mississippi state president of the NAACP, and Ruby Hurley, the southeast regional secretary who worked from the Birmingham, Alabama, office, arrived in Belzoni as soon as they could.

The local police had already "investigated" the murder and ruled Lee's death a simple auto accident. Those lead pellets in his jaw? Those were dental fillings, said the Belzoni police.

But when two black physicians looked at the body, they confirmed that the lead in Lee's jaw did indeed come from a gun, and they also found pellets in the tire of the car.

Faced with this new evidence, Ike Shelton revised his police department's story to smear Lee's reputation. The sheriff claimed that the reverend was having extramarital affairs and was killed by a romantic rival—playing to the myth of blacks being oversexed and violent. Shelton's deputies swooped down to patrol the black section of town, and any witnesses who contradicted Shelton's "official" story were silenced.

Lee's death was especially distressing to Medgar Evers. This was someone he knew personally, someone who shared his dream. Evers was angry that, once again, the murder of a black would go unpunished. But all he could do was brood silently or rage at the injustice of the affair, usually to Myrlie. Evers' job was to help people in need, and when he couldn't help, he took it personally.

Reverend George Lee's name had been on the

When one of Evers' colleagues, the Reverend George Lee, was murdered in Belzoni, Mississippi, Ruby Hurley, the southeast regional secretary of the NAACP, drove from Birmingham to be with Evers, who was especially distressed by Lee's death.

so-called "death list," a full-page ad in the Delta newspaper that listed nine prominent black leaders. The list was circulated among the White Citizens' Councils, and now with Lee dead the list had eight names left.

One of those names was Medgar Evers.

Because of his NAACP activities in the Delta, Evers' car and license plate number were well-known to local lawmen. They would watch him closely and even follow him in their cruisers. This was meant as a warning; if they had wanted to kill him, they could have done so in a snap and gotten away scot-free. Sometimes, Evers and his NAACP associates would have to disguise themselves as poor sharecroppers when they traveled in the Delta.

He had so much to be concerned about by now that he had no time to worry about his personal safety. There was the Lee investigation, the school desegregation petition drive, voter registration drives, urging people not to remove their names from petitions, sending relevant newspaper clippings to the NAACP national office, sending loan applications to the Tri-State Bank, and, as always, investigating every incident of racial trouble that he could. But Myrlie, remaining at the office with a phone hot with obscenities and threats, could not be so detached. Every time Medgar left the office, she feared that she would never see him alive again. She said later, "It was about this time that I began trying to live each day for itself, to count as special blessings those days when I knew he was in no special danger...; the only alternative was some kind of breakdown."

After a year and a half on the job, Evers thought he had seen it all. But it would become even worse in late summer of 1955.

On August, 20, 1955, a fourteen-year-old black boy from Chicago named Emmett Till got on a southbound train. He was going to visit relatives in Money, Mississippi, a tiny town located in the Delta. Emmett's traveling companion was his seventeen-year-old cousin, Curtis Jones, whose grandparents lived in Money. Emmett's family was one of the many who had migrated from Mississippi to Chicago. Now, the boy was going to take a good look at his roots.

Emmett's mother had warned him to "mind his manners" with white people while in Mississippi, but "manners" had a different definition in Mississippi than in Chicago. During that summer, there had been an alarming increase in white murders of blacks, which coincided with blacks' growing political boldness. But Emmett Till was not thinking about this when he got off the train in Mississippi. He was young, it was summer, and he was looking to have fun.

Curtis Jones' grandfather, Mose Wright, was

a preacher, and inevitably the whole family would go to church to hear him in the pulpit. But Emmett and Curtis had more interesting ideas. They sneaked out of the church and drove back to Money. They went into the general store to stock up on candy. Emmett found some black boys of his own age and showed them a picture of his integrated class at school. He also said— probably fancifully—that one of the white girls was his sweetheart.

One of the boys then dared him to speak to a white woman in the store. He went inside, bought more candy, and, according to Curtis Jones, said "Bye, baby" to the white woman as he left. It was hardly the best example of "manners," but it was still an innocuous episode. Then, Curtis and Emmett went back to church to hear the end of Mose Wright's sermon.

News of this incident quickly spread among the black youth in the town, and they warned Emmett and Curtis to leave as soon as possible, before the woman's husband found out. But days passed without the threatened retribution, and the boys let it pass out of mind.

Then, one week later, a knock came at the door of Mose Wright in the wee hours of the morning. When Mr. Wright opened the door, he saw two white men. They asked for the boy "that did all the talking." Mrs. Wright protested, but she was struck in the head with the side of a shotgun. Then, the men took Emmett away. Four days later, his body was found at the bottom of the Tallahatchie river.

This was not a case of simple drowning. Emmett Till had been stripped naked, beaten, shot through the head with a .45 caliber automatic, then had a seventy-five-pound cotton gin fan tied around his neck with barbed wire. He could be identified only by the ring on his left hand.

Mamie Till Bradley, Emmett's mother, intercepted the body before it was buried and decided that the family's privacy was less important than revealing this atrocity to the world. Emmett's casket was left open, and a photo was printed in *Jet* magazine.

The sight of Emmett Till's mutilated body not only shocked blacks, it drew white attention as well. Even whites normally indifferent to racial problems were appalled at this particularly brutal murder of a child. Unlike George Lee's murder, the Till case became a pan-racial, nationwide issue. Newsreel and TV cameras swarmed around the Delta. The white-hot glare of publicity shone on Mississippi, and even the most diehard racists squirmed.

The death of Emmett Till brought tears to the eyes of Medgar Evers, despite his belief that men were not supposed to cry. Emmett Till's fate could befall his children—if nothing was done.

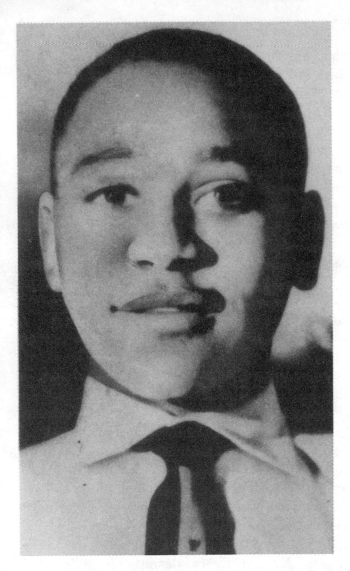

Emmett Till, visiting the Mississippi Delta from Chicago, bragged to friends that he had a white girl friend back home, whereupon they dared him to "say something" to a white woman in a rural store. He went inside, bought some candy and said, "Bye baby,"

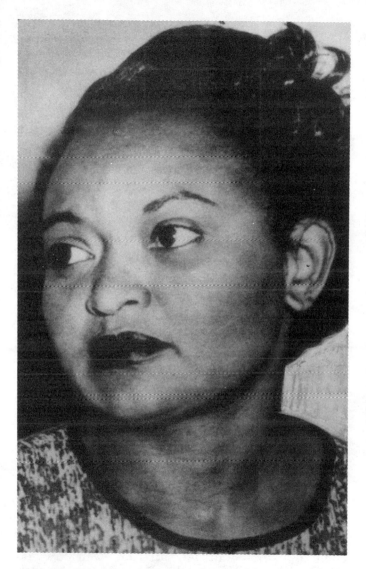

as he left. A week later he was murdered and four days after that his body was found in a river. His mother, Mamie Till Bradley, decided that the family's privacy was less important than letting the world see what had been done to her son.

Evers ferried witnesses to Memphis, where they were flown out-of-state for their safety until the trial, which was scheduled for September 19, 1955.

Two men, J.W. Milam and his half-brother, Roy Bryant, were arrested for the murder. The tipoff came from a white reporter from Jacksonville, Florida, who pointed out that a gin fan, because it left a unique set of grooves in a cotton gin, could be traced to a specific machine. The fan tied to Emmett Till was traced to Milam's barn.

Milam and Bryant were tried in a segregated courtroom in Sumner. Blacks were not allowed to stand in the halls or sit anywhere in the court, and the jury was all-white. It was not a sympathetic atmosphere.

Mose Wright, who had seen the two men who had abducted Emmett, had insisted on testifying, despite the danger to himself. The prosecutor, referring to this sixty-four-year-old man as "Uncle Mose," asked if two men came to Mose Wright's house asking for "a nigger here from Chicago." Mr. Wright said that they did, and they took Emmett with them. Then the prosecutor asked if Mr. Wright could see any man who came to his house in the courtroom that day. Mr. Wright looked around, pointed right at J.W. Milam, and said "Dar he!" The judge had to quickly restore order in the court after Mose

Alabama native William Bradford Huie, author of They Slew
The Dreamer *and other books on the civil rights movement, got
the slayers of Emmett Till to confess—in detail—to the crime.*

Wright's heroic act.

But despite this identification, the evidence of the gin fan, and eyewitness reports, the jury acquitted Milam and Bryant after only one hour of deliberation.

Two months later, William Bradford Huie, a white journalist from Alabama, interviewed Milam and Bradley. The men admitted that they were indeed the ones who took Emmett Till from his granduncle's house. Not only that, Milam said that he shot Emmett in the head. They did not intend to kill the boy when they took him, but when Emmett—probably babbling out of fear—said that he had a white girlfriend in Chicago, Milam and Bradley knew what they had to do. Milam said, "[White women are] what we got to fight to protect."

Look magazine published Huie's interview in January 1956. Because of the Constitution's prohibition on double jeopardy, there was nothing the law could do now. But ironically, Milam and Bryant were ostracized for "disgracing" their community for their well-publicized act.

The Emmett Till case was a turning point not only for Mississippi but for the nation as well. The cloak of darkness—that is, mainstream media inattention—was now lifted on the uglier manifestations of Mississippi racism. White men would continue to get away with the murders of blacks—but not without protest from both blacks and whites.

Hodding Carter, the editor of the white newspaper *Delta Democrat-Times,* said of the Till case: "Mississippi gave a sorry demonstration of an inadequate legal system...that presented an attitude of so little concern that even the people most convinced that two half-brothers were guilty of murdering a young Negro boy from Chicago, had to admit that the case was not proved."

Carter compared the Till murder to another case that was tried in Sumner, in which a black gas-station employee, Clinton Melton, was shot in broad daylight by a white customer who had complained that Melton didn't put enough gas in his car. This white man was also acquitted, despite eyewitness testimony. This case "served to cement the opinion of the world," continued Carter, "that no matter how strong the evidence nor how flagrant the apparent crime, a white man cannot be convicted in Mississippi for killing a Negro."

Medgar Evers and the NAACP had known that for years.

Chapter Seven

Mississippi
and Murder

TO FURTHER PUBLICIZE the Emmett Till and George Lee murders, the NAACP published a tiny eight-page booklet entitled *M is for Mississippi and Murder*. This booklet contained quotes from racists and segregationists predicting that interracial bloodshed would be the only logical result of the *Brown* decision. A Yazoo *Herald* editorial blamed Emmett Till's death on the Supreme Court, not the two men who killed him: "Some of the young Negro's blood is on [the Court's] hands, too."

A Delta legislator said that "a few killings" would be good for Mississippi, evidently as a

James Coleman as governor of Mississippi in 1957. He was as anti-civil rights as Ross Barnett had been and was the attorney general who rejected Evers' application to Ole Miss Law School.

means to set an example for blacks and scare them away from activism.

John C. Satterfield, the president of the Mississippi Bar Association, said that an "abhorrent" but possibly necessary means of continuing segregation was the "gun and torch."

Dr. A.B. McCoy, the Mississippi president of the NAACP, was also blamed for the violence. "If not suppressed by his own race," said Frederick Sullens, editor of the Jackson *Daily News,* "[McCoy] will become the white man's problem." Sullens characterized McCoy's words against segregation as nothing more than "fanatical mouthings."

If nothing else, this booklet gave an interesting look at the amazing ability of racists to twist the truth like a pretzel, at how they would rationalize murder and brutality in order to preserve their system.

Clearly, these people and thousands like them were not about to give up their way of life without a good fight. By now, Medgar Evers was used to fights. The question remained as to whether he would come out alive.

The "gun and torch" were not the only weapons used against blacks in Mississippi. In the mid-1950s, the state legislature wrote a proposed amendment to the Mississippi Constitution requiring all registered voters to be able to read or write any part of the state constitution and give an interpretation thereof to the county registrar. Although this amendment made no mention of race, blacks would be more affected than whites because most blacks, especially in rural areas, were poorly educated.

The proponents of this amendment admitted that it was meant to "check the increasing number of Negro ballots," but in reality black registration was 22,404 in 1954—or only four percent of the adult population. The number who actually voted was even less.

Nevertheless, voters were concerned enough to approve this amendment in November 1954. In March of the following year, another law was passed that nullified all voter registrations since January 1, 1954—a law that made no sense except to purge the rolls of black voters. This law wiped out much of the work of Medgar Evers and the NAACP in that area.

The man who became governor in 1956, James P. Coleman, was not going to give assistance to the NAACP. Coleman was the former attorney general who had played a key role in keeping Medgar Evers out of the University of Mississippi. In his inaugural speech, Coleman promised blacks that he would give a sympathetic ear "to any of your problems which desire the assistance of the state government," but also warned, "If you reject [this opportunity], the responsibility is yours." He also assured the citizenry that "when my successor stands on this same spot to assume his official oath, the separation of the races will be left intact...."

Two months after Coleman's ominous speech, nineteen southern senators and seventy-eight southern congressmen—including Mississippi's entire delegation—wrote the so-called "Southern Manifesto," which condemned the *Brown* decision and praised states that defied the Supreme Court.

Medgar Evers' response to this was to set up voter registration drives, hoping to get these Southern Manifesto writers removed from office. But NAACP membership and contributions dropped in Mississippi, mainly because of economic intimidation. The national office had to step in with emergency relief to save branches in Natchez, Indianola, Yazoo City, and Greenville. It was like taking one step forward and two steps back.

The president of the United States during this time (1952-60) was Dwight D. Eisenhower. Eisenhower was no outspoken racist, but he was also no outspoken ally of the foes of racism. He was the president who sent National Guard troops to Little Rock, Arkansas, to make sure that black children could safely attend a newly integrated high school, but that revealed more a commitment to law than to social justice. Eisenhower talked obliquely of the need to

President Dwight Eisenhower was the president who sent the National Guard troops to protect the black children entering Little Rock's Central High School as students for the first time.

change men's minds and hearts before changing laws and criticized "extremists on both sides."

This was a full decade before the more radical fringe of the civil rights movement came into flower. Medgar Evers wondered: was it extreme to register and attempt to vote, as the *written* law permitted? Was it extreme to petition for schools to be desegregated at once, as the Supreme Court had ordered? Was it extreme to want a happy, peaceful life with the same freedoms and opportunities as the majority?

During World War II, Evers had served under General Eisenhower. Now it was time for the soldier to lead the general. When Eisenhower announced plans to invite Soviet Union leaders to view America's "free" elections, Evers and his NAACP cohorts wrote a letter to the White House reminding Eisenhower that elections were not free in all places and for all people. They urged Eisenhower to show the Soviets Humphreys County, Mississippi, where George Lee had been murdered and Gus Courts, president of the Belzoni NAACP branch, had been shot because they tried to vote. Mississippi's terror campaign could rival anything that was going on in communist Russia.

Two years later, in 1958, Evers wrote an even stronger letter to the President: "As a former soldier under your command in the European Theater of Operations..., I hereby urge you, as

President and Chief Executive of the United States, the greatest democracy on earth, to speak out vigorously in urging national compliance with the Supreme Court rulings of 1954 and 1955 as regards to segregation."

The closest he ever got to an answer was this note from a member of the White House staff: "The President is always pleased to hear from any soldier who served under his command. He faces current problems of this country with the same courage he faced similar problems during the war, and he will meet them with his best judgment and determination." It might as well have been a form letter.

The idea of "buying black"—that is, blacks supporting black entrepreneurship with purchasing dollars—became a weapon in the fight for rights. Medgar Evers encouraged his friends and family to go out of their way to patronize black-owned businesses. When Myrlie said that the local Kroger's, a white-owned grocery chain, had a greater selection and lower prices, Medgar replied, "But they wouldn't hire you as a checker."

So the Everses purchased their groceries at the Valley Street Grocery, owned by a father-and-son team, Reverend Robert Smith and Robert, Jr. Because of black support, the Smiths' grocery grew into a full-scale supermarket by 1960. The Smiths became close friends of the

Everses, as did Houston Wells, a furniture-store owner. Evers admired these black entrepreneurs who, like himself, were industrious and ambitious men serving their community.

Most white-owned stores on Capitol Street, Jackson's shopping district, did not turn away black customers; money was money. But blacks were not guaranteed respectful service. They were usually waited on only after all the white customers in the store had been helped. They were not allowed to try on clothes, and they were called by their first names instead of "Mr.," "Mrs.," or "Miss." Once, a saleswoman refused to allow Myrlie to try on a hat without stuffing tissue in it because blacks had "greasy hair."

The Everses also selected a black physician, Dr. A.B. Britton, as their family doctor. In his office, they did not have to use a separate waiting room or go in through a side entrance. When Myrlie had to see a white dentist, she noticed that no other patients were in the waiting room. The dentist explained that he scheduled all his appointments so that patients would wait alone—avoiding the problem of segregated waiting rooms. The dentist believed that segregation was wrong but didn't feel that he could be open about it. Many of his co-tenants in the office building were members of the White Citizens' Council.

The white dentist was far from the only one

The bus station in downtown Jackson, Mississipi. It, like several others across the state and throughout the South, was the scene of sit-ins and demonstrations during the civil rights era.

of his race who was unhappy with the "way things were." But, except for an outspoken few who were dismissed as eccentric, these uneasy whites kept their silence. The racists made much more noise, and when they were crossed they could get very nasty. They would ruin an "unsympathetic" white's livelihood just as soon as they would ruin a black's. Fear and practicality too often kept dissenting voices of both races silent.

By now, Medgar Evers had outgrown his Mau Mau fantasies and harbored no hatred toward white people as a group. He understood that their thoughts and behavior were shaped by the influences they grew up with. The racists did not know better because they were not taught better. Evers' anger was reserved for those who murdered and brutalized and those who allowed them to get away with it.

He worked hard not to allow his children to grow up as ill-informed. When young Darrell, upset over a news program, said that he hated white people, Medgar reminded him that it was not good to hate, because it did nothing but destroy the person who did the hating. Medgar knew that hard-core racists, those who wasted precious energy on hatred, could never be truly happy people.

In the 1950s, Evers befriended a young man named Clyde Kennard, who worked for the

Medgar Evers realized that the most important right that blacks had to acquire was the right to vote, and so he concentrated his efforts on voter registration drives. Once they had a voice in their country, they could gain other constitutional rights.

Hattiesburg NAACP youth program. Evers found that he had much in common with Kennard, who had lived in Chicago for a while, was an army war veteran (having served in Korea), and had attended college (at the University of Chicago). Only his stepfather's disability had prevented Kennard from earning his degree, and he had returned to Hattiesburg to work on the family farm.

A short drive away from Kennard's farm was the University of Southern Mississippi, a whites-only institution. Kennard decided that he wanted to attend USM—not to make a point against segregation but simply because it was the school nearest to him and he wanted to finally earn his degree. Kennard even rejected legal help from the NAACP, saying the USM was more "liberal" than other schools—although he had applied three times without formal reply.

One day in 1959, Dr. William McCain, USM's president, came to Kennard's farm and told him that Governor Coleman wanted to see him. The two went down to Jackson, where Coleman met with them privately.

Coleman said that although Kennard was qualified to attend USM, it would not be a good idea for him to apply *now* because the primary elections were coming up and Coleman didn't want controversy to mar the campaign of his handpicked successor. Coleman also asked if

Kennard would attend any other college in the nation, with the state footing the bill. Kennard reiterated that he preferred to attend USM but agreed to delay his application.

After the primaries—in which Coleman's candidate lost anyway—Kennard applied to USM once again. In a letter to the Hattiesburg *American*, Kennard explained why segregation was inherently evil. "The more segregation and discrimination we have in our community, the more we shall have ignorance and immorality," he wrote, referring to the high crime rate in black communities. "Teach men to do a job and then give them the job to do, and high morality will follow as the day follows the night."

Kennard also urged government and private employers to make room for educated blacks: "If there are to be no jobs in government, science, or industry, in vain is time and money spent educating the child...; what part will the educated Negro play in our society in future years?"

When it came time for his formal interview at USM in September 1959, Kennard discovered that his application had been rejected for three reasons: Kennard did not submit his transcript from the University of Chicago; he turned in a "forged" medical certificate (actually, he had updated the calendar dates from a previous application); he had been refused readmittance to the University of Chicago (which was untrue).

A dejected Kennard returned to his car and walked right into a setup. He was arrested for reckless driving, and at police headquarters one of the arresting officers produced a bottle of liquor which, he said, had been found in Kennard's car. Possession of liquor was illegal in Mississippi at that time, but that bottle did not belong to Kennard, who was a non-drinker.

Nevertheless, he was charged with both reckless driving and liquor possession. He had to pay $600 bond to leave the jail, and his car was impounded. Kennard was quickly convicted and fined an additional $600, a hardship for a struggling farmer.

Still, Kennard planned to continue his fight to get into USM. And Forrest County realized it had to do more than convict Kennard of a misdemeanor in order to stop him. He had to be framed for a felony, which would automatically disqualify him from attending any Mississippi college.

On September 25, 1960, Johnny Lee Roberts, a nineteen-year-old black, stole five bags of chicken feed from the Forrest County Co-op warehouse, where he worked, and hid them in Kennard's chicken house. The police arrested Kennard at 8:30 A.M., although they did not start to search for the stolen feed until noon.

On the witness stand, Roberts said that not only was Kennard an accomplice to the burglary, he had planned it all and bribed Roberts to steal the feed. However, Roberts gave confused testimony as to when and how Kennard plotted the crime, despite prompting from District Attorney James Finch.

As usual, the jury was all-white. And once again, it came down on the side of white interests. Kennard and Roberts were both found guilty, but while Roberts was given five years' probation (and promptly rehired by the feed warehouse), Kennard was sentenced to the maximum seven-year prison term, to be served in hard labor at the Mississippi State Penitentiary in Parchman.

Kennard did not win release until 1963, and then only after reports in black-oriented publications and Medgar Evers' publicity efforts threatened to embarrass the state. But he was released too late to save his life; that summer, he succumbed to cancer in Chicago.

Clyde Kennard, an intelligent, articulate black man of potential, had been treated as a common criminal by his home state. His faith that reason alone would defeat segregation had been betrayed. Foolishly, Mississippi continued to squander valuable human resources in the form of gifted black men and women.

Medgar Evers and the NAACP realized that the 1950s were just a time of getting started. The 1960s were the time to get serious.

Chapter Eight

Progress

THE MIDDLE 1950s to early 1960s were watershed days for civil rights progress in the South. It was the era of the Montgomery bus boycotts, the integration confrontation at Little Rock's Central High, and the emergence of Dr. Martin Luther King and his non-violent philosophy. College students devised the "sit-in," in which civil rights workers would sit quietly at drugstore lunch counters. This took seats away from paying white customers and eventually left store owners with no choice but to integrate. Black students entered the Universities of Alabama and Georgia for the first time. All

Dr. Martin Luther King emerged with his non-violent philosophy soon after the integration of Little Rock's Central High and students devised the "sit-ins" to begin the "rights" movement.

across the South, blacks realized that they *could* act to change their world, that there were other ways to deal with racism besides acquiescence.

It took a person of formidable mental strength to face tales of murder, rape, and police brutality without sinking into despair. It also took a person of great patience—not patience that was willing to wait indefinitely for change, but the ability to remain calm in the most stressful situations. Fortunately for himself and the NAACP, Medgar Evers was that person.

Calls poured into the Jackson NAACP office and the Evers home, but not all of them were from people asking for help. Crank calls and obscenity-spewers would frequently tie up the line. Myrlie remembered a call from a drunken woman asking Medgar if he was "the head nigger of that NAACP or whatever you call it?"

"The head what?" asked Medgar.

"The head *nigger!*"

"Well, if you want to call me that, yes," he replied politely.

It would no doubt have been unprofessional for the state field secretary of the NAACP to get into a screaming match with an ignorant crank, but Evers' equilibrium was a part of his personality.

He knew that his job was dangerous as it was; he didn't need to be careless. He took reasonable precautions to protect himself and his family and left the rest to fate.

The threat of danger dictated the large and small events in the Everses' lives. Medgar bought a new car in 1962, not because it looked nice but because he needed a faster car to keep far ahead of anyone who wanted to follow him.

When they bought their house on Guynes Street, which was in a subdivision built by a black-owned company, the position of the house was important. Medgar and Myrlie considered a house, larger than the rest, on a street corner. A corner house, however, would be more exposed to possible attack and easier for a potential assassin to get away from, so instead, they bought a smaller house nestled between two others.

The Everses had several guns in the house and one in the car. Medgar warned Myrlie to always pull the car into the driveway and to exit it on the right side, not the left as was usual, so as to avoid being seen clearly from the vacant lot across the street. They also alternated cars to further confuse people trying to follow Medgar.

The children did not attend the Jackson public schools, which were segregated. Instead, Darrell and Rena (another son, James Van Dyke, was born in January 1960) were sent to a Catholic school, Christ the King, despite the Everses' Baptist religion. The teachers, white nuns, protected the children well.

What Medgar Evers had sought a few years before, acceptance to study law at the University of Mississippi, James Meredith gained in September 1962, though it took not only a court

order but the presence of federal marshals to escort him onto the Ole Miss campus. Previously, Mississippi Governor Ross Barnett personally blocked Meredith's enrollment.

Medgar Evers was a father who spent quality time with his children and enjoyed it. He also taught them the troubled history of blacks in America without giving a blanket condemnation of whites.

When the danger got closer to home, Medgar taught the children to listen for any extraordinary sound and to drop to the floor until it was safe to get up. They looked at this as kind of game. When Medgar asked them where the safest place in the house would be, they searched the house and decided that the bathtub, well-fortified and hidden, was it.

Myrlie did not think of this as fun and games. Teaching children how to defend themselves in case of gunfire should not be necessary in the United States of America, she thought. What was most disturbing, she remembered, was "the enemy here was not a foreign power but [fellow] American citizens."

Medgar received some much-needed support from the national NAACP office in June 1961. Roy Wilkins, then the president of the NAACP, announced the launch of "Operation Mississippi," whose goal was to "wipe out segregation in all phases of Mississippi life."

Operation Mississippi, according to the NAACP master plan, would be fought in the courts. Two Jackson businessmen filed suit in federal court against the public transportation system. Another suit was filed against voting registrars in Clarke and Forrest counties. And another suit had begun that had important ramifications for the future of the state.

All James Meredith wanted was the best education possible. To that end, he served nine years in a now-desegregated U.S. Air Force, accumulating college credits in the meantime. After his tour of duty, Meredith enrolled at Jackson State, but that was not enough of a challenge. Like most Mississippians, James Meredith considered the state's *best* college to be the University of Mississippi. And he determined that he would earn his bachelor's degree there. But he soon found out that it took more than good grades and money to go to Ole Miss. When he first applied in February 1961, he was rejected.

With the might of the NAACP legal team behind him, Meredith filed suit in U.S. District Court, charging that he was denied admission "solely because of his race." The battle to get Meredith enrolled would take sixteen months and cost the state millions, much of the blame belonging to new Mississippi Governor Ross Barnett, who had promised that no black would attend Ole Miss as long as he was in office and said that if the university was integrated, it would be nothing less than "genocide."

In February 1962, Judge S.C. Mize of the U.S. District Court denied that "qualified Negroes" were barred from the university due to "custom or policy." Though no blacks attended Ole Miss, Mize asserted that "the university is not a racially segregated institution."

Meredith turned to the U.S. Fifth Circuit Court of Appeals, where, by a two-to-one majority, it was ordered that he be admitted. Judge John M. Wisdom accused the university of using "a...campaign of delay, harassment, and masterly inactivity" to keep Meredith out.

But no court could tell Mississippi what to do. On September 20 and 25, Meredith tried to apply and was turned away. Barnett, holding fast to his promise, appointed himself university registrar and personally blocked the Ole Miss gate on September 26, backed by four hundred officers of the law.

The Kennedy administration was furious with Barnett's "states' rights" stubbornness. The Justice Department declared him in contempt of court and then threatened to jail him unless he gave the go-ahead for Meredith's admission.

Evidently, Barnett's resolve crumbled in the face of possible jail time. On September 30, 1962, a Sunday, James Meredith was escorted onto the campus at Oxford by federal marshals. Hundreds of fire marshals, border patrolmen, and prison guards were stationed to protect him. It was necessary to have that many protectors, because two thousand people stormed the campus, throwing rocks and Molotov cocktails. The police responded with tear gas. By the time the riot died down, two people were dead and 160 injured—all because one person wanted to attend the college of his choice.

James Meredith survived the riot and harassment from other students, to graduate in August 1963. He went on to law school and a career furthering the good of the black community. He once mused, "If one places society above self, and I do, life never ends. Everything I do, I do because I must, and everything I must do, I do."

Medgar Evers couldn't have been happier about Meredith's achievement if *he* had been the one to go to Ole Miss. And why not? Meredith had fulfilled Evers' dream of eight years before.

In the early 1960s, new groups rose up in Mississippi to join the NAACP in the civil rights battle. The Student Non-Violent Coordinating Committee (SNCC), which organized the early sit-ins, and the Congress of Racial Equality (CORE) sent field secretaries into Mississippi. The Southern Christian Leadership Conference (SCLC), founded by Martin Luther King, Jr., also had a presence in the state.

Amzie Moore, the vice-president of the state conference of the NAACP, said this about the younger groups: "Every time [the NAACP] moved, we moved according to law.... But when SNCC came in, SNCC moved in SNCC's way."

SNCC's way was more personally active than filing lawsuits. Volunteers placed themselves between prospective voters and violence-mongers in McComb, and faced arrest when they marched on McComb City Hall to protest the suspicious killing of Herbert Lee. Lee had accused State Representative E.D. Hurst of taking down the license-plate numbers of blacks who registered to vote; Hurst said that Lee came after him with a tire-iron and he had to shoot in self-defense.

Medgar's attitude toward these groups was ambivalent at first. He was of course happy with the extra help; all of the groups were working toward the same goal. But his point of view was biased toward the NAACP. The NAACP was still the oldest group, it had been in Mississippi first, it had a sterling reputation for helping through legal means, and it was the group *he* belonged to. Evers wrote a small booklet trumpeting the accomplishments of the NAACP when it appeared that the newer groups were siphoning away much-needed donations.

But when he learned of the courage of SNCC workers in McComb, he felt ashamed at the relative inaction in Jackson, the NAACP hub. Evers wondered if maybe the NAACP's *modus operandi* of going to court was strong enough. The Mississippi backlash against civil rights was becoming more violent, and while he did not

At first Medgar Evers felt the student sit-in movement would be detrimental to his NAACP work, but he realized that segregation had to be attacked on all fronts and he worked with others such as John Lewis (above) of SNCC to achieve common goals.

think counterattack was the answer he felt that the NAACP's approach of patience and prudence was limited and slow.

When Evers asked for the national NAACP office's support for the sit-ins and marches, he was given a polite refusal. An invitation to Martin Luther King to visit Mississippi was also discouraged. The NAACP would move in the NAACP's way. A frustrated Evers was determined to do something different—even if it meant leaving the NAACP altogether. The various civil rights organizations did find enough common ground to band into the Council of Federated Organizations (COFO) in 1962, although each group retained its distinct name and identity. The COFO quickly received some much-needed federal aid in the form of the Voter Education Project, which enabled it to expand its drive into western Mississippi and the Delta. Still, progress was slow.

Medgar Evers was being pulled in many directions—by the COFO voter registration drive, by his everyday NAACP work and meetings, by his children who depended on him, by Myrlie who secretly wished he would find another line of work, by the ever-present specter of death. But none of these forces could pull him off the forward path. The time to act was now—he had no time to worry about whether there would be a tomorrow.

Between 1961 and 1964, blacks began to attack segregation in all its forms, from denial of education and voting rights to seating in restaurants and movie theaters. Above is a demonstration in Washington protesting lack of federal employment of blacks.

Chapter Nine

Hope

MAY AND JUNE OF 1963 were two of the most active and productive months of Medgar Evers' life. They were also the last.

Evers urged blacks to boycott Barq's soft drinks, Hart's bread, and McRae's department store because of their economic support of White Citizens' Councils. Eventually, the entire Capitol Street shopping district was targeted, and business there suffered.

The Mississippi NAACP got tougher regarding city hiring practices. On May 12, it demanded that Jackson Mayor Allen Thompson appoint a biracial committee to end discrimination in the

---

During the spring of 1963 the eyes of the nation were on Mississippi as civil rights efforts were stepped up. In June, an NAACP rally in Jackson attracted celebrities such as Lena Horne.

hiring of police officers, firemen, and other city personnel.

Thompson refused outright. In a speech heard on both radio and television, he claimed that such a move would divide the city even more, that it would be "compliance with the demands of racial agitators from outside."

Evers demanded equal time on local television to reply to Thompson's remarks—and, to his surprise, he got it. On May 20, the face and voice of Medgar Evers visited Mississippi living rooms, black and white.

Evers said that the NAACP was not a group of "outside agitators," having been present in Mississippi for more than forty years. He talked about the role of the U.S. Supreme Court in breaking down segregation laws and declaring non-violent demonstrations legal. Evers also said that it would take more than time to end Mississippi's racial crisis, which had festered for hundreds of years.

"[The] years of change are upon us," he declared. "In the racial picture things will never be as they once were.... Here in Jackson we can recognize the situation and make an honest effort to bring fresh ideas and new methods to bear, or we can have what Mayor Thompson called 'turbulent times.'"

Evers gave an articulate, totally reasonable speech, one which urged rapprochement, not separation. It was a revelation to many white Mississippians who had never heard a black man talk like this before. Many whites became a bit more cordial to blacks after the speech, and some even took down the "Whites Only" signs at their stores.

Myrlie was proud—and worried. Not only did people hear her husband speak, they also saw his face. Now many Mississippians knew what he looked like—including those who wanted to end his crusade. *They* were still out there.

The day after his speech, Evers sent Mayor Thompson a telegram containing the names of fourteen black leaders, including himself, for the proposed biracial committee. Thompson countered with his own list of blacks who were more sympathetic to his point of view, including Percy Greene, who had written the infamous "The Voice of A Negro" editorial, and Sidney Tharp, a lawyer who had written a letter to the Jackson *Daily News* praising Thompson's stand against the NAACP. The two lists had only four names in common, and those four immediately refused to work with Thompson because his list had not been chosen by the black community.

On May 28, Thompson met with an NAACP committee and agreed on several points:

1. Blacks would be hired as policemen and school crossing guards;

2. All public facilities would be open to all cit-

izens and "Whites Only" signs taken down;

3. All city officials would use courtesy titles (Mr., Mrs., Miss) when addressing blacks.

But Thompson insisted he could do nothing to desegregate lunch counters and public schools. Those were matters for the state government.

The NAACP and blacks in Jackson barely started to celebrate this announcement when Thompson denied it all, saying that he had been "misrepresented." The mayor also banned demonstrations in the city.

The black community had long been used to bitter disappointments, but Thompson's reneging on his agreement was the last straw. This could not go unanswered.

That afternoon, people began sit-ins. At the F.W. Woolworth store, four black male students and a white professor from Tougaloo Southern Christian College and three young white women sat at a whites-only lunch counter. Counter-demonstrators poured condiments like ketchup and sugar on the heads of the sitters, but they did not budge. One of the black students, Memphis Norman, was dragged from his stool and kicked in the face. The culprit, a former Jackson policeman, was eventually sentenced to thirty days in jail.

When black students at Lanier and Brinkley High Schools walked out of class in response to an order from the principals not to demonstrate, the police came in to literally beat the students back into class. Some of the students fought back with bottles and bricks. The news excited the black youth of Jackson, and they were eager to march in protest.

Medgar had mixed feelings about demonstrations. He knew that they brought needed publicity to the civil rights cause, but he also feared that if taunts and abuse got to the demonstrators, tempers could flare and demonstrations could degenerate into riots.

But the kids had to do *something*, so Willie Ludden, the NAACP youth field secretary, was summoned to organize them. A date was set for May 31, and definite starting and finishing points were decided upon.

About six hundred students participated, filling up Capitol Street. The police force, sheriff's deputies, and highway patrolmen closed in after three blocks of marching. They sandwiched the marchers on both sides and hurled them into police wagons, construction trucks, and even garbage trucks. Since the regular jails were already overcrowded from the previous day's arrests, the youngsters were sent to the "temporary" jail—the animal stables of the state fairgrounds.

Despite the dirty, crowded conditions, the students remained in high spirits, singing songs, making speeches, and pledging not to accept bail, because that meant promising never to demonstrate again. Some spent more than a week in the stables before their worried parents could retrieve them. But the majority believed that the ordeal had been worth it. One young man, commenting that he had not brushed his teeth in a week, said joyfully, "Look, Mom, cavities for freedom!"

Medgar was moved by the courage of these youngsters and thought that if they picketed, so should he, so he and Roy Wilkins joined the march on Capitol Street on June 1, and, like the students, they were arrested almost immediately. This time, the NAACP came up with $1000 bail for each. It could not afford to have its executive director and Mississippi field secretary sit in jail for a week.

On the midnight of the sit-in demonstrations, Medgar was at the Pearl Street A.M.E. (African Methodist Episcopal) Church leading a rally. At home, the children slept while Myrlie waited for him to come home. A passing car threw something at the Evers house, and it smashed. Myrlie thought it was just another bottle at first, but it turned out to be a firebomb, which turned the carport into a sheet of flame.

Before putting out the blaze, Myrlie called Thomas Young, a neighbor, and asked if the perpetrators were still outside, waiting to do more damage. But she could not wait for the reply;

the fire was getting dangerously close to the gas tank of the parked car. She put out the fire with a garden hose.

When the fire was out, a police car appeared on the scene. Neighbor Jean Young had called Medgar, and Medgar had called the police. Soon after, he came home and asked Myrlie if the children were all right. Surprisingly, they had slept through it all.

One of the policemen reassured the Everses that, "There's nothing to worry about. It was just some kind of prank." Later that night, the impact of the incident came in full force—this was an assassination attempt. Myrlie became terribly frightened at the possibility of life without Medgar. "It's you they're after," she said. "And if anything happened to you, I don't think I could live."

Medgar embraced her, but that did little to ease Myrlie's fears. Never before had widowhood come so close.

The stepped-up activity in Jackson meant a jump in Evers' workload. Days at the NAACP office started at 7:00 A.M. and lasted until the wee hours of the morning, seven days a week. The phones at the office and at home rang constantly. Once, a radio station in Chicago called Evers at 3:00 A.M. for an interview. He dutifully complied but had forgotten what he had said by the morning. The small details of life began to escape him. He even put his pants over his pajama bottoms one morning.

Myrlie seriously feared for Medgar's health. He now looked like a man many years older than thirty-seven. He would not complain about his workload, but she resented those who thoughtlessly demanded more and more of his time. Only she knew just how stressed he was. On June 7, the Masonic Temple in Jackson was crammed with 3,500 people for an NAACP rally. Police surrounded the building, but no skirmishes occurred, despite growing confrontation in the city and 664 arrests since May 28.

The rally started with the singing of what had become the anthem of the civil rights movement, "We Shall Overcome." Entertainer Lena Horne sang spiritual songs and told the crowd that they were lucky to have Medgar Evers as their leader. She had gotten acquainted with him when he had picked her up at the airport. Comedian/activist Dick Gregory, who had been in Jackson earlier to picket, also spoke. Gregory's participation was even more remarkable because of the recent death of his infant son, Richard, Jr. But he knew that this movement could not stop for grief. Medgar was the final speaker of the evening. Along with the usual news of upcoming events and the appeal for donations came an admonishment: "It's not enough just to sit there tonight...and clap your

At the civil rights rally in Jackson in June, Claude Hudson of the Los Angeles branch of the NAACP was one of the speakers, as were Lena Horne and Dick Gregory (at right), who participated despite the fact that he was mourning the recent death of his son.

hands and shed your tears and sing and then go out and do nothing about this struggle. Freedom has never been free.... There is something for everybody to do."

And then he said, "I love my children, and I love my wife with all my heart. And I would die, and die gladly, if that would make a better life for them."

Myrlie knew that he truly meant it. But these were words she did not want to hear. Medgar was more than a man now; he was a symbol of hope for thousands who had not dared to hope before. And, she realized sadly, he was now something more important than husband to her and father to Darrell, Rena, and Van.

After that meeting, Medgar Evers spoke more about death. He told Myrlie out of the blue that he should renew his life insurance policy, even though they could not afford the premiums. He asked her to promise to look after the children if anything happened to him. When she told him to stop such morbid talk, he replied, "You shouldn't be afraid of death, honey..., it's something that comes to everyone someday."

The morning of June 12, Myrlie woke up early to iron a week's worth of shirts for Medgar. He appreciated this gesture but said, "I'm not going to need them."

That night, he attended a mass meeting at the New Jerusalem Baptist Church. While

Medgar was away, Myrlie and the children stayed up late to watch a televised speech by President Kennedy. The subject was civil rights, and Kennedy was direct: if America paid no attention to skin color when drafting troops for Vietnam, why should it care about color at the public schools or ballot box? There was no time for Eisenhower-like fence-sitting: "Who among us would then be content with the counsels of patience and delay?" The case for equality was a mortal one. "We cannot say to ten percent of the population...that your children can't have the chance to develop whatever talents they have.... I think we owe them and we owe ourselves a better country than that...."

At this time, Medgar was driving Gloster Current home from the meeting. "I'm tired," he said to Current. "I want to get home to my family."

After the speech, the children continued to watch TV until they heard the crunch of car wheels against the gravel in the driveway.

"Here comes Daddy," cried Darrell.

As they rose to greet him, the shots rang out. As they had been taught to do, Myrlie and the children fell to the floor.

Friends and family swarmed to the Evers home. The two older children alternated between disbelief and tears. The three-year-old Van kept asking "Daddy's gone?," too young to understand permanence.

Myrlie's aunt came over as soon as possible, and so did Charles Evers. True to his childhood potential, he had become active in business in the 1950s and 1960s, holding jobs as a radio disc jockey, a funeral-home director, and owner of the first black-owned taxicab company in Philadelphia (Miss.). At the time of Medgar's death, Charles owned a tavern in Chicago.

It was Charles who would inherit the job of NAACP Mississippi field secretary, a job he kept until he was elected mayor of Fayetteville in 1968. Charles said that he and Medgar had made a promise—no matter what, there always had to be an Evers in Mississippi, fighting the good fight.

Medgar Evers' funeral took place on June 15 at the Masonic Temple, the same building in which he had spoken of the price of freedom. He had said earlier that he did not want an elaborate, costly funeral. "When I'm gone, I'm gone, and I won't know a thing about it," he had said.

It was one wish that was not granted. Four thousand people packed the sweltering auditorium, doubtless including many people who only knew him through newspapers. Attendees included Dr. Martin Luther King, Ralph Bunche, Roy Wilkins, and Dr. T.R.M. Howard. The casket was left open, despite Myrlie's request that it be closed.

The funeral procession was followed by a march of mourners. Today, the Jackson police had given permission to march. The mourners surrounded the Collins Funeral Home, old and young, those who had been "with" the NAACP for years and those who had only now found the courage to show their support publicly.

Grief turned to anger as someone shouted, "Capitol Street!," and the younger members of the group literally ran toward that destination. The police retreated at first, then met the crowd of about one thousand head-on. Deputy Police Chief A.L. Ray sternly reminded the crowd of the agreement to march peacefully.

The crowd was not ready to talk peace. They threw bottles and bricks, screaming, "We want freedom! We want the killer!" The situation rapidly deteriorated as the police brought out their dogs and their guns. Some of the protesters dared the police to shoot.

Then John Doar, a Justice Department attorney, walked into this developing riot. He had worked in Alabama and Mississippi for two years, and he had enlisted Medgar Evers' help while investigating voting discrimination in 1961. Doar had been impressed with Evers' knowledge of exactly what was happening in almost every county in the state. Now it was time for Doar to pay Evers back.

An angry black man pointed a gun at Doar's

head, but Dave Dennis, cofounder of COFO, talked the gunman away from the scene. A policeman gave Doar a bullhorn, and the crowd looked skeptically at this white man in a dress shirt and tie. Who was he, and what could he tell them about justice?

"You're not going to win anything with bottles and bricks," he said. "Medgar Evers wouldn't want it this way."

The crowd gradually calmed down, knowing that Doar was right. A riot was not a fitting memorial for Medgar Evers, a man who shunned violent confrontation.

Evers was supposed to be buried in the black cemetery in Jackson, but the American Veterans Committee—where Evers had served on the board—suggested that he be buried instead at Arlington National Cemetery in Virginia, the resting place of presidents and heroes. Myrlie was surprised by this offer, but she accepted.

The body was placed on a train to Washington, D.C., and was met by representatives of all the major civil rights organizations and thousands of mourners. Myrlie, Charles, and the children arrived by plane. Twenty-five thousand people viewed the body in a Washington funeral home.

June 19 was the date of the final burial. As the procession drove toward the cemetery, Myrlie was amazed at the thousands of people who lined the streets, black and white people sharing grief. It was then that she realized that her husband was a hero not only to Mississippi but to the entire nation.

The graveside was just the kind of place that Medgar Evers would love—green, fresh, and peaceful, shaded by trees. Just like the countryside of the state he loved so well and would not leave except in death.

Mickey Levine of the American Veterans Committee made it clear why Evers was being buried here: "No soldier in this field has fought more courageously, more heroically than Medgar Evers.... We shall go to the Congress, we shall go to the people; he shall not have died in vain."

The Evers family met President Kennedy at the White House the next day. Darrell and Rena were awed by it all, but Myrlie, though touched by Kennedy's words of sympathy, knew that this was an honor she could have done without, given the price she and the children had to pay for it.

When they returned to Jackson, they discovered that its new airport was open for business— and it was fully integrated. Medgar Evers had fought to desegregate the old airport but had only achieved a partial victory in the restaurants, which quickly built reserved sections for whites only.

Chapter Ten

Quest for Justice

O<small>N</small> JUNE 23, ELEVEN days after the assassination of Medgar Evers, a suspect was arrested.

Byron de la Beckwith, age forty-two, was a tobacco and fertilizer salesman who had been born in California but who lived in Greenwood, a Delta town. He was a White Citizens' Council member and had a habit of writing letters espousing his segregationist views to newspapers, including this gem: "When you get to heaven, you will find me in the part that has a sign saying 'for whites only,' and if I go to Hades I'm going to raise hell all over Hades until I get to

Medgar Evers was given numerous honors posthumously. Among them was a special Veterans' Award, which Myrlie Evers accepted from Ralph Bunche, Undersecretary of the United Nations.

the white section."

Beckwith was also a collector of guns. A recent addition to his collection was an Enfield 30.10 rifle, which was the exact same type of rifle found in the honeysuckle bush across the street from Evers' house. When Jackson police captain Ralph Hargrove dusted it off for fingerprints, he found one near-perfect print of an index finger on the telescopic sight. That fingerprint was discovered to belong to Beckwith.

Friends and acquaintances called Myrlie and told her that Beckwith was one of three white men who mysteriously appeared at an NAACP rally the Friday before Evers was killed. These men were not recognized as reporters or supporters, and they had poked around the office suspiciously after the rally was over.

Myrlie could not be relieved when the arrest was made. She knew Mississippi history all too well, and she considered it unlikely that Beckwith would serve a day in prison. She was surprised when Beckwith was indicted and given a trial date of January 27, 1964.

The district attorney, William Waller, did not inspire confidence as far as Myrlie was concerned. He was an avowed segregationist, and he told Myrlie that he did not approve of Medgar's actions. Still, he promised to do his best to prosecute Beckwith.

When Myrlie expressed concern that she

would be called by her first name on the witness stand, Waller asked why that was such an important matter to her. Myrlie replied, "This is one of the things that my husband lived and fought for. If it is a question of winning the case or my being called 'Mrs. Evers,' well, I have lost a husband for those principles, and I refuse to lose my dignity and pride, too."

Beckwith had three lawyers on his side. His expenses were paid by a White Citizens' Legal Fund, which had little trouble raising thousands of dollars for Beckwith's defense. As usual, the jury consisted of twelve white men. Each of them was asked by District Attorney Waller—in these exact words—"Do you believe that it is a crime to kill a nigger in Mississippi?"

Neither Waller nor Hardy Lott, one of Beckwith's attorneys, referred to her by name, avoiding both the offensive "Myrlie" and the unthinkable "Mrs. Evers." Lott asked questions about Medgar's application to Ole Miss and Darrell's middle name, Kenyatta, which had nothing to do with the case and obviously served to make Medgar look like a militant radical. Judge Leon Hendrick sustained Waller's objection to that line of questioning.

Witnesses had seen Beckwith's car, a white 1961 Valiant, driving slowly around the vacant lot across from the Evers house the night before the murder. Two taxi drivers waiting in front of

When the NAACP awarded its Spingarn Medal to Medgar Evers, Myrlie accepted it with dignity, accompanied by the two older Evers children, Rena (left) and Darrell (right). Van was too

young to attend the ceremonies, which took place at the 54th annual convention of the NAACP in Chicago in July, less than a month after Medgar was slain by an assassin's bullet.

the Jackson bus station remembered Beckwith coming up to them and asking where "Nigra Medgar Evers" lived. FBI agents noticed a circular scar above Beckwith's eye that could have come only from a Goldenhawk telescopic sight— the part of the rifle where Beckwith's fingerprint was found.

When Beckwith himself took the stand, he did not behave like a wrongly accused man. He said firmly that he did not kill Medgar Evers but did not account for his whereabouts on the night of June 12, 1963. He admitted to owning an Enfield 30.10 rifle but claimed it had been stolen shortly before the murder. He did not disavow his race-obsessed letters.

On February 6, ten days after the trial began, the jury began deliberating the fate of Byron de la Beckwith. At that time, a murder conviction in Mississippi meant an automatic death penalty. In the history of the state, no white man had ever been executed for murdering a black.

After a surprising two days of deliberation— most people expected a speedy acquittal—the jury declared that it could not unanimously decide Beckwith's guilt or innocence, and a mistrial was declared. That meant that some white Mississippi men on the jury thought that Beckwith *was* guilty of murder.

A second trial was set for April, and it was almost an exact reenactment of the first. Once again, the jury was deadlocked; once again, there was a mistrial. Beckwith was released on $10,000 bond. In 1969, all charges against him were dropped.

And that, it seemed, was the end of the Medgar Evers case.

Civil rights progress marched on, literally as well as figuratively. Two months after Evers' death, the March on Washington brought 200,000 people to the nation's capital, where they heard Martin Luther King's now-legendary "I Have A Dream" speech. King was the best-known civil rights leader in the 1960s, and his non-violent yet steadfast philosophy gained wide admiration among blacks and whites. King had faith that "history is on the side of justice." But mounting violence and frustration gave birth to other philosophies, other leaders.

Ironically, some of these individuals and groups repudiated Evers' ideal of an integrated society, saying that blacks could flourish only outside the circle of white influence. Stokely Carmichael (later Kwame Toure), who coined the term "black power," and the Nation of Islam advocated black solidarity, not black assimilation. Malcolm X, the best-known member of the Nation of Islam, once likened white people to "devils" who oppressed the superior black race. Although Malcolm would become more tolerant in the last years of his life, his words were not lost on young blacks who were grasping for self-esteem.

On July 2, 1964, President Lyndon Johnson signed the Civil Rights Act of 1964, which had been developed by his predecessor, John F. Kennedy. The Act finally placed federal laws on the books prohibiting discrimination in employment and federally assisted programs. It authorized the U.S. Attorney General to desegregate public facilities, including schools, and established a four-year Commission on Civil Rights. In August 1965, Johnson signed a bill that buttressed voting rights. No longer could individual voting registrars turn blacks away from the polls. Medgar Evers' most important battle had been won at last.

Despite these gains, the years 1964 to 1968 were filled with civil unrest in America's cities. Frustrated blacks, believing that they could do nothing else, took out their anger on their neighborhoods. The flames of riots burned high in the summertime, the worst of which occurred in Los Angeles (August 11-18, 1965, with thirty-four killed) and Detroit (July 23-31, 1967, with forty-three killed). Violence broke out in thirty U.S. cities after the assassination of Martin Luther King in April 1968.

As for Mississippi, the violence would get worse before it got better. The COFO's "Freedom Summer" project of 1964 brought hundreds of

The Evers home on Guynes Street in Jackson has been given to Tougaloo Southern Christian College to be used as a museum. Some of the students from Tougaloo, a historically black college, were active in the sit-ins in Jackson in the 1960s.

college students to the South to volunteer in voter registration and education. This idealistic project ended in tragedy when three of the volunteers, James Chaney, Andrew Goodman, and Michael Schwerner, were shot to death and buried in a dam. Ku Klux Klansmen were eventually jailed for the murders. The triple murder outraged the nation and, along with the Evers assassination, dirtied Mississippi's reputation even further.

The majority of Mississippians may have accepted segregation but not the violence that raged to preserve it. Ole Miss alumni were horrified at the damage to the campus during the Meredith riots. More people were thinking that enough was enough.

Economic pressure on the state also kept the heat on. The federal government threatened to cut off money, chain-business owners threatened to leave the state, and fewer groups wanted to hold conventions and other events in Mississippi.

Governor Paul B. Johnson, elected in 1963, told his constituents, "You and I are part of this world, whether we like it or not.... National policies have a direct bearing on our economy, on our political freedom, and our daily living...." It was time for Mississippi to join the United States of America.

The schools began to be desegregated at last,

although some districts, including Jackson, did it with one grade per year. Cities began to hire black policemen. And the "white" and "colored" signs began to come down for good. Mississippi and the other southern states at last belonged to *all* of their citizens.

Many hands worked to make that dream possible. But few had worked harder than Medgar Evers. He loved his home state and only wanted to make it a little better. He knew that change never happened overnight, that it had to begin within the individual. Those people he touched— the friends who voted with him, the sharecroppers whom he clothed and fed, the witnesses he protected, the terrified parents he encouraged to fight for their children's futures, the young people he inspired to march, the thousands of people who attended his mass meetings—learned through his example. That lesson is one that transcends decades.

In 1964, Myrlie Evers and her children moved to Claremont, California. She maintained a career as a public speaker on civil rights and wrote a number of magazine articles. In 1967, she and William Peters wrote a book entitled *For Us, the Living*, the story of her life with Medgar. Myrlie went to work for the Los Angeles Commission of Public Works. Although she remarried, she continued to use the surname Evers as both tribute and reminder.

In 1989, Bobby DeLaughter, the assistant district attorney of Jackson, was taking a closer look at the Medgar Evers case twenty years after it was closed. He had discovered through Jerry Mitchell, a reporter for the Jackson *Clarion-Ledger*, that the Mississippi Sovereignty Commission, which was designed to uphold segregation policy in the 1960s, had deliberately excluded blacks and Jews from the jury at the second trial. This jury tampering could be grounds for Byron de la Beckwith to be tried again.

DeLaughter looked for the transcripts of the trial, but they could not be found in either the district attorney's or circuit clerk's offices. Then, Myrlie Evers sent DeLaughter copies of the transcript from the first trial. She had been given the transcripts by William Waller and had kept them in a safe deposit box for years.

The Enfield rifle, which had mysteriously disappeared after the second trial, was found, in all places, at the home of DeLaughter's former father-in-law, a local judge.

The transcripts and the rifle, however, were not enough to justify a retrial. *New* evidence was needed—and an obscure 1975 book provided it.

Klandestine, written by John Birch Society member William McIlhany, was the story of Delmar Dennis, a former Ku Klux Klansman turned FBI informant. He recalled that

Beckwith admitted killing Evers at a Klan meeting. Beckwith asserted chillingly, "Killing that nigger gave me no more inner discomfort than our wives endure when they give birth to our children. We ask them to do that for us. We should do just as much."

New witnesses came forward, witnesses who were afraid to speak in 1964, fearing the loss of jobs and even life. One of these witnesses was the grocer, Robert L.T. Smith. These witnesses said that Beckwith was not in Greenwood, which is over ninety miles away from Jackson, the night before the assassination as he had said. They saw Beckwith at Medgar Evers' last rally in Jackson.

Because the autopsy report was also missing from the case files, a new one had to be performed. That meant exhuming Evers' body from Arlington Cemetery and establishing anew that he had died of a gunshot wound.

In December 1990, a grand jury reviewed the evidence, old and new, presented by DeLaughter and returned an indictment against Beckwith. At that time Beckwith, age seventy, was living in Signal Mountain, Tennessee. He still insisted he had not killed Evers, even as he was extradited to Jackson and held at the Hinds County Detention Center without bail.

When the prospect of a new Beckwith trial came up, Myrilie Evers stated: "I look at what is happening today in our society and I see a retraction of all of these things that Medgar worked so hard for," she said. "I live with [his memory] every day, the good memories, the encouragement, the wisdom that he had, as well as the negative of losing him...."

More than thirty years from the day he had been arrested for the assassination of Medgar Evers, Byron de la Beckwith was convicted of the crime at last. The trial showed just how far race relations had come in Mississippi—and raised intriguing questions about why today's justice system reaches the verdicts that it does.

On February 5, 1994, after a total of six hours' deliberation, a jury in Jackson decided that enough evidence had been presented in the six-day trial to prove that Beckwith was indeed the triggerman. Hinds County Circuit Judge L. Breland Hilburn sentenced Beckwith to life in prison, the mandatory sentence for murder under Mississippi law, although Beckwith could be paroled in ten years.

The jury for this third trial was quite different from the two that had deadlocked on Beckwith in 1964. Those juries, as custom dictated, consisted entirely of white men. Now, eight blacks and four whites served. The jurors came from Panola County, 140 miles north of Jackson.

Surprisingly, it wasn't hard to find jurors who

knew little, if anything at all, about Medgar Evers.

There were those, black and white, who questioned the value of a third Beckwith trial. So much time had passed, they said. Beckwith was now an old man; why bother putting him in jail? Why bring back these bad memories?

Morris Dees, executive director of the Southern Poverty Law Center in Montgomery, Alabama, and an expert on racial hate crimes, said that reopening the case was important not only for blacks but for all Americans. "It's always important that a person who commits murder be punished.... It doesn't matter whether the murder in question was committed thirty years ago or yesterday, the passage of time does not diminish guilt."

The prosecution's case was predicated on testimony that Beckwith, ever since he had been set free in 1964, had improvidently boasted of killing Evers. One woman, Mary Ann Adams, stated that Beckwith had been introduced to her in 1966 as "the man who killed Medgar Evers," an appellation Beckwith did not deny. When Adams refused to shake his hand, Beckwith insisted he had not killed a man but a "damn chicken-stealing dog."

When Beckwith was serving time in Louisiana in 1979 for an attempted bombing, he had shouted to a black nurse that if he could "get rid of

DEDICATED
TO THE MEMORY OF
MEDGAR WILEY EVER
BORN JULY 2, 1925
DECATUR, MISS.
ASSASSINATED JUNE 12, 1
JACKSON, MISS.

FIELD SECRETARY MISSISSI
STATE CONFERENCE OF N.A.
BRANCHES 1954 — 1963
ERECTED JULY 4, 1969
BY MISSISSIPPI STATE CONFER
NATIONAL ASSOCIATION FOR
ADVANCEMENT OF COLORED PI

On July 4, 1969, the Mississippi State Conference of the NAACP erected a memorial in Jackson to the memory of Medgar Evers, who was the organization's first Mississippi field secretary.

This time the youngest Evers child, Van, was able to attend.
He is seen at left, standing in front of his sister Rena.
Darrell is at right with Myrlie Evers, Medgar's widow.

an uppity nigger like Medgar Evers, I would have no problem with a no-account nigger like you."

Beckwith, however, still maintained in court that he didn't shoot Evers, although he wasn't sorry to see him dead. Now seventy-three, he gave the appearance of a frail old man and declined to testify himself because of—he claimed—a fading memory. But those who knew him said that he was as alert as ever—and still a diehard racist.

The defense, now as before, depended upon the testimony of two Greenwood, Mississippi, police officers that they had seen Beckwith at a gas station in their town, ninety miles away from Jackson, an hour before Evers was killed. But only one of the officers, James Holley, testified in person at the third trial. The other, Hollis Cresswell, was too ill to appear.

Civil rights supporters had dismissed this story as a cover-up by two racist cops who were probably just as happy to see Evers dead as Beckwith was. But Holley said that although he had been pro-segregation in 1963—like "just about every white person in the state," according to defense attorney Jim Kitchens—he now lived in an integrated neighborhood and had no problem with living among blacks. But Holley proved to be a less-than-credible witness. He had once claimed to be Beckwith's good friend, having known him since the 1940s, but in 1994 he said, "There were very few times I ever talked to the man."

Also, there was the question of why neither Holley nor Cresswell reported the Greenwood sighting to anyone other than Beckwith's attorney at the time, while Beckwith spent seven months in jail awaiting his first trial. Even if Holley and Beckwith were not friends, was there not a moral duty to prevent an innocent man from being jailed for murder? "No police officer ever asked me," was the reply, which evidently did little to sway the jury to Beckwith's side.

The trial came to a bizarre close when Kitchens called for a mistrial because of the withholding of testimony from a prosecution witness. That witness was Martha Jean O'Brien, who had claimed in 1964 that she had seen a car parked outside the Evers home that was similar to Beckwith's. The prosecution, unable to locate Mrs. O'Brien, instead read her previous testimony.

But Kitchens claimed that a woman saying that she was Mrs. O'Brien had called him the day before jury deliberations. He accused the prosecutors, District Attorney Ed Peters and Assistant District Attorney Bobby DeLaughter, of keeping Mrs. O'Brien off the stand because they thought she was too old and frail to withstand cross-examination. Judge Hilburn, however, said that any motion on a mistrial would have to wait until after the verdict.

The jury itself made little comment after the verdict, except for the statement of the foreman, Rev. Elvage Fondren, that the jury had little trouble reaching its decision. "I believe [Evers'] wife and family got justice," said Fondren. So, many believed, did Mississippi.

But did it get relief as well? A short deliberation was rare in murder cases, except when evidence of guilt or innocence was definitive. "Definitive" was not quite the word for the third Beckwith trial. Aside from the Enfield rifle and Beckwith's fingerprints, the prosecution's case rested on the words and memories of those who had encountered Beckwith—and human words and memories are not infallible. None of these people had actually seen the assassination. Even Martha Jean O'Brien's testimony, live or not, was only about the car and not the shooting.

Some people speculate that more than one person was involved in the Evers murder—a conclusion easy to come to in these conspiracy-mongering times, and even more so given the racism-choked thicket of 1963 Mississippi. They believe Beckwith knew about the crime but allowed someone else to use his weapon—a logical explanation for his approval of—but denial of committing—the crime.

The verdict was a dream come true for Myrlie

Evers and her children. Even though the years had vindicated her husband's message, even though she had reared three children, remarried, and become Los Angeles' Commissioner of Public Works, something was missing in her life: justice and, with it, closure of an open wound.

"What I wanted, needed, prayed for...was to hear the jury say, 'guilty.' Medgar's life was not in vain," Myrlie Evers said with tears in her eyes. Later she looked up at the sky—finding her late husband, no doubt—and declared, "Medgar, I've gone the last mile of the way."

It was she who had prodded the State of Mississippi to reopen this politically disturbing case. She attended each day of the trial, along with two of her children, Darrell and Rena. They, like their mother, were also seeking peace.

Darrell said, "The main reason I wanted to be there is because...I wanted [Beckwith] to see my father looking at him." Some believe that Darrell bears a strong resemblance to Medgar. "I stared at him, and we had a big stare down.... That was the only way I could reach out and touch that man."

"Going back was scary," said Rena, who named her eldest son Daniel Medgar Evers Everett. "It was real painful. I [had been] able [before] to escape a lot of feelings that had been locked inside.... [But] I had to go back for me. I wanted to open that door, let it out, and then hopefully close the door."

Although unable to attend the trial with his mother and siblings, Van, the youngest, also played a significant role. He helped inspect Medgar's body when it was exhumed in 1992.

Van had been only three years old when his father had been killed and therefore did not have the opportunity to know him as well as Darrell and Rena had. It may seem strange, but Van was happy about attending the exhumation. "I never got a good look at my father. To see him was as much a joyful release as the trial. I got to meet him up close, face to face."

Although the Evers children were inevitably pressured to continue their father's legacy of civil rights activism, they have succeeded in living happy and productive lives—and that, after all, was what Medgar Evers wanted people of all races to be able to do.

This story does not end with the verdict. As Beckwith's lawyers prepared their appeal, the name of Medgar Evers burned brighter than ever. Myrlie says she has received countless pieces of mail from those who are also celebrating the verdict. A Mississippi state highway has been named for Medgar, as well as a branch of the City College of New York in Brooklyn.

The Evers family has also donated the home where Medgar died to Tougaloo College, which plans to turn it into a museum.

It would have saddened Medgar Evers to see the problems that have begun to face blacks in America now that the battle he fought for equal rights has been won—the gangs, drugs, teenage pregnancy, family dysfunction, and violence. Many attempt to blame the woes of blacks on racism, poverty, lack of job opportunities, poor education, welfare, rap music, and/or the decline of religion.

It is easier to blame than it is to take a good look at oneself and then take action for positive change. Medgar Evers lived a life that was arguably more difficult from the outside than many do today. Yet he did not pick up a gun, don the "colors" of a gang, or refuse to make something of his life just because other people said he wasn't supposed to. Even in the worst of circumstances, the human spirit can spin gold. That is just one of the many reasons why Medgar Evers must always remain part of our history.

CHRONOLOGY

1925   Medgar Wiley Evers born, July 2, at
       Decatur, Mississippi.
1942   Drops out of high school to join army.
1946   Attempts to register to vote; denied.
1947   Succeeds in voting in county election;
       returns to finish high school.
1948   Enrolls at Alcorn State University.
1951   Marries Myrlie Beasley on Christmas Eve.
1952   Listed in *Who's Who in American Colleges*;
       graduates from Alcorn; begins working for
       Magnolia Mutual Insurance Company;
       begins recruiting members for NAACP.
1953   Birth of son Darrell Kenyatta Evers; begins
       voter registration drives.
1954   Birth of daughter Rena Evers; attempt to
       enroll at Ole Miss Law School denied; hired
       as first NAACP Field Secretary for
       Mississippi.
1960   Birth of son James Van Dyke Evers.
1961   NAACP's "Operation Mississippi" begins.
1963   Assassinated on June 12.

INDEX

187

188

PICTURE CREDITS

Florida State Archives: p. 17; Library of Congress: pp. 13, 15, 20-21, 39, 55, 72-73, 85, 87, 91, 100-101, 105, 110, 111, 116, 121, 127, 136-137, 145, 146, 162; Ray Locke: pp. 11, 24, 27, 44, 46-47, 62, 68-69, 78, 113, 125, 171; Medgar Evers College: pp. 8, 29, 32-33, 53, 96, 143; Courtesy of NAACP Public Relations: pp. 81, 93, 155, 166-167, 178-179; James Neyland: pp. 37, 51; Players International Archives: p. 132.

Melrose Square Publishing has made every effort to reach the copyright holders of all the photographs reproduced in this book.